English for Emails

SHORT COURSE
SERIES

Verfasserin   Rebecca Chapman, Vienna

kritische Durchsicht   Paul Abbot, Berlin
                           JoAnne Meise, Minneapolis
                           Nisar Zaker, Ingolstadt

Verlagsredaktion   Janan Barksdale
Redaktionelle Mitarbeit   Christine House, Fritz Preuss (Wortliste), Claire Wingfield
Design/Herstellung   Sylvia Lang
Bildredaktion   Uta Hübner

Bildquellen   Titel: Corbis Düsseldorf/W. Schick
                           Illustrationen: Oxford Designers & Illustrators
                           Fotos: COMSTOCK, Luxemburg: S. 13, 17, 23, 31, 47;
                           Das Fotoarchiv, Essen: S. 40/M. Vollmer; Getty Images, München: S. 26/T. Vine,
                           S. 37/S. McClymont; Getty Digitalvision: S. 5, 18, 25, 33, 43

Weitere Titel in der *Short Course Series*:
English for Accounting Bestell.-Nr. 18806
English for the Automobile Industry Bestell.-Nr. 18776

 http://www.cornelsen.de

Die Internet-Adressen und -Dateien, die in diesem Lehrwerk angegeben sind, wurden vor
Drucklegung geprüft (Stand: März 2003). Der Verlag übernimmt keine Gewähr für die Aktualität
und den Inhalt dieser Adressen und Dateien oder solcher, die mit ihnen verlinkt sind.

1. Auflage   Druck 4 3 2 1   Jahr 06 05 04 03

Alle Drucke dieser Auflage sind inhaltlich unverändert
und können im Unterricht nebeneinander verwendet werden.

Druck: CS-Druck CornelsenStürtz, Berlin

ISBN 3-464-01878-4

Bestellnummer 18784

 Gedruckt auf säurefreiem Papier,
umweltschonend hergestellt aus chlorfrei gebleichten Faserstoffen.

Inhalt

Vorwort

In den letzten Jahren sind E-Mails Bestandteil unseres Lebens geworden und eine der häufigsten Kommunikationsformen im heutigen Berufsleben. Da ein großer Teil der Korrespondenz in Englisch ist – ob intern mit Kollegen oder extern mit Geschäftspartnern und Kunden – sind bestimmte Kenntnisse für das Schreiben von E-Mails *auf Englisch* unverzichtbar.

English for Emails wird Ihnen helfen, sich diese Kenntnisse anzueignen.

English for Emails besteht aus sechs Units, die die unterschiedlichen Aspekte des Verfassens von E-Mails behandeln. Jede Unit enthält vielfältige Übungen, die Ihnen helfen neue Ausdrücke zu lernen und in Ihre E-Mails zu integrieren. Der **Answer key** im Anhang erlaubt Ihnen Ihre Antworten zu überprüfen und selbstständig zu arbeiten. Wenn Sie mit den Units fertig sind, haben Sie die Möglichkeit Ihre Kenntnisse mit einem Kreuzworträtsel zu überprüfen, in dem das Vokabular des SHORT COURSE wiederholt wird – **Test yourself!**

Am Anfang und am Ende jeder Unit finden Sie eine **Inbox** bzw. eine **Outbox**. Die **Inbox** enthält kurze Übungen oder Fragebögen, die bestimmte Aspekte der E-Mail-Kultur verdeutlichen. In der **Outbox** werden fakultative Lese- und Diskussionsübungen zum Themenkreis E-Mail angeboten.

Am Ende jeder Unit werden Sie auf den Abschnitt **You've got mail!** im Anhang verwiesen. Diese Rollenspielszenarien geben Ihnen die Möglichkeit E-Mails mit einem Partner auszutauschen, sodass Sie die Ausdrücke und Wörter situativ anwenden können, die Sie in der Unit gelernt haben.

Der Anhang enthält darüber hinaus eine hilfreiche **A–Z wordlist** und eine Zusammenstellung von **Useful phrases and vocabulary** zum Nachschlagen nach Ihrem E-Mail SHORT COURSE, wenn Sie wieder an Ihrem Arbeitsplatz sind.

An introduction to emails

What do you think about emails?
Make a cross on the scale to represent how much you agree
(5 = I agree 100%) or disagree (0 = I disagree 100%).

1 You need the same language skills to write an email as you do to write a letter.

agree | 5 | 4 | 3 | 2 | 1 | 0 | disagree

2 If you can *speak* English well, you can write good emails.

agree | 5 | 4 | 3 | 2 | 1 | 0 | disagree

3 One of the most important features of an email is the subject line.

agree | 5 | 4 | 3 | 2 | 1 | 0 | disagree

4 Accuracy is still very important when writing emails.

agree | 5 | 4 | 3 | 2 | 1 | 0 | disagree

5 Using the 'cc' option is a great way to inform others who are not directly involved.

agree | 5 | 4 | 3 | 2 | 1 | 0 | disagree

6 One reason for emailing is to reduce the response time.

agree | 5 | 4 | 3 | 2 | 1 | 0 | disagree

7 If you need an answer straight away, it is better to use the phone than send an email.

agree | 5 | 4 | 3 | 2 | 1 | 0 | disagree

Discuss your answers with a colleague and/or check the key.

1   Label the screen with the following English equivalents.

attachment @ contacts @ deleted items @ drafts @ forward @ high priority @
inbox @ outbox @ reply @ reply to all @ send/receive @ sent items @ subject

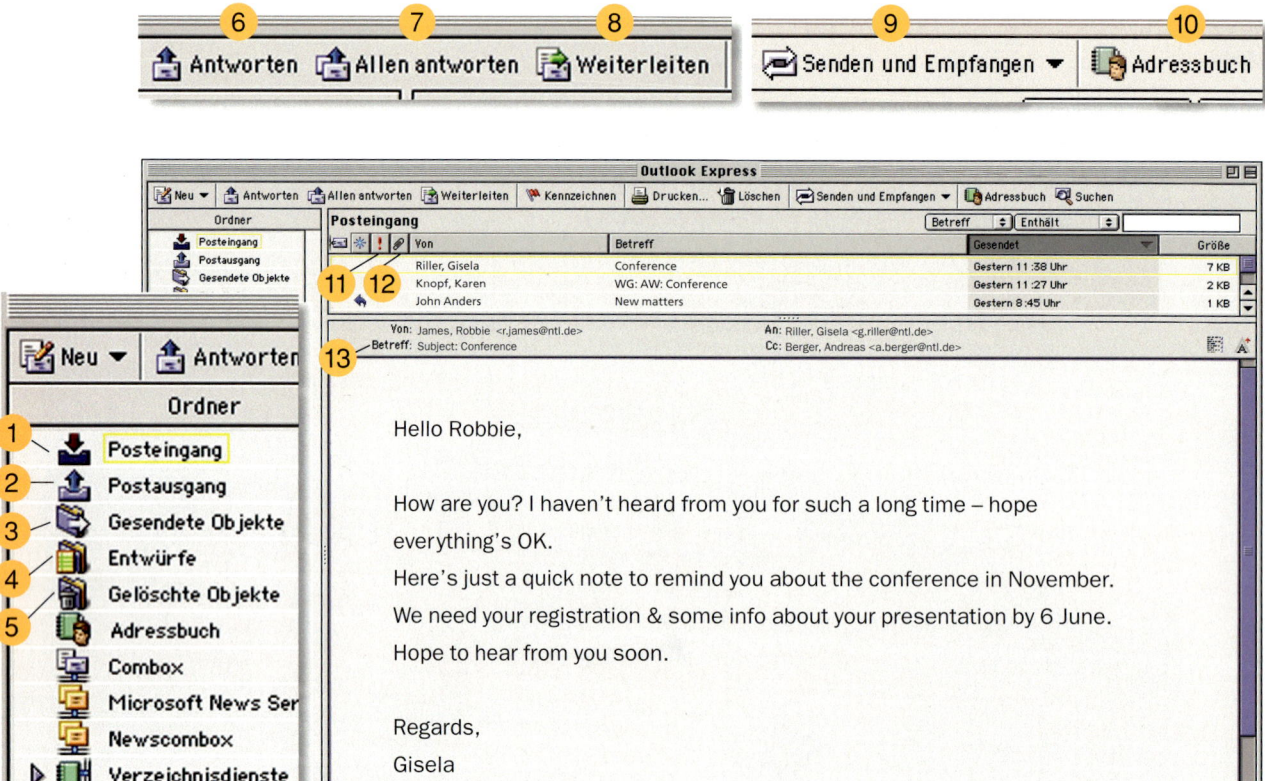

2   Where or how can you do the following?

1   Find old emails you have sent.
2   Find emails you have received.
3   Send an email you have received to a third person.
4   Find email addresses and other personal data.
5   Put emails you are working on but are not yet ready to send.
6   See what a message is about.
7   Show that an email is important and should be read immediately.
8   Find a document which has been sent with the email.

3   Now look at the message. Find five things that make it different from a letter.

 **TIP** | **Email structure**

One of the advantages of emails over normal 'snail-mail' letters is that they are quick and direct. We send an email for a particular purpose and we expect a fast response or immediate action. For emails – whether formal or informal – to be most effective, it is a good idea to give them a clear, logical structure.

Subject line: This should be short and give some specific information about the contents of your message.

Salutations: As in letter-writing, the salutation can be formal or informal, depending on how well you know the person you are writing to.

Dear Mr, Mrs, Ms ...	*A formal form of address, also used when first contacting a person.*
Dear John	*Less formal. Either you have had contact with this person before, or they have already addressed you by your first name.*
Hi/Hello Mary (or just the name)	*Informal, usually used with colleagues you often work with. In the USA and the UK also sometimes used at first contact.*
(no salutation)	*Very informal, usually used in messages which are part of a longer email exchange.*

Opening sentence: This is used to explain why you are writing. (Remember: the opening sentence should always start with a capital letter.)

I'm writing to ...	*More formal introduction to say why you are writing.*
Just a quick note to ...	*Friendly, informal way to say why you are writing.*

Conclusion: This is where you tell the reader what kind of response, if any, you expect.

Looking forward to your reply.	*Friendly ending, can be used in formal or informal correspondence.*
Hope to hear from you soon.	*Informal ending to indicate a reply is necessary.*

Close: Like the salutation, this can vary from formal to very informal.

Yours sincerely	*Very formal, rarely used in email correspondence.*
Regards/Best wishes	*Most commonly used close, can be used in formal and informal emails.*
Bye/All the Best/Best	*Friendly, informal close.*
James/Mary	*Name only (or initials) is also common when writing to close colleagues.*

4 **Look at this excerpt from a typical inbox and find an email ...**

from Martin which ...
1 is urgent.
2 is probably not work-related.
3 is asking for input.
4 contains new information about a meeting.
5 is a reply to an email you sent.

from Julia which ...
6 is a request for information.
7 was sent on from someone else.
8 contains one or several documents.
9 contains information about the new division.

			Von	Betreff	Gesendet	
				Posteingang	an ⬍ Enthält ⬍	
a			Martin Weber	ideas for a venue?	05.03.2003 12:34	
b			Martin Weber	sales meeting	05.03.2003 13:36	
c		📎	Martin Weber	something amusing for you	05.03.2003 13:53	
d			Martin Weber	car park closed tomorrow	05.03.2003 15:34	
e	!		Martin Weber	sales meeting update	05.03.2003 17:41	
f			Martin Weber	Re: tomorrow's event	05.03.2003 19:34	
g	↩		Meadows, Julia	outstanding invoices	06.03.2003 09:02	
h	!		Meadows, Julia	FW: invoice 0167	06.03.2003 09:55	
i			Meadows, Julia	REQ: current price list	06.03.2003 12:38	
j			Meadows, Julia	Info	06.03.2003 16:49	
k			Meadows, Julia	Info	07.03.2003 11:06	
l		📎	Meadows, Julia	PET contract	07.03.2003 11:45	

5 **Did you have trouble answering number 9? That's because Julia's subject lines don't always give enough information about the contents of her emails.**
Look at the following excerpts from emails and write appropriate subject lines.

1 Subject: _____
Just a quick note to see if you've heard from Production about the new schedule. We need the info for tomorrow's meeting.

2 Subject: _____
Many thanks for your email. The handbook for the XL20 motor is now available online at www.hardysgardensupplies.com.

3 Subject: _____
I will be away from the office from 3–5 October. Please direct all questions to Maggie in my absence.

4 Subject: _____
I have to change our meeting to 3 pm instead of 12.00. Sorry!

5 Subject: _____
Could you send me those staff guidelines asap? Our dept hasn't seen them yet. Thx.

6 Subject: _____
I am writing to confirm your order of 1000 coffee mugs with logo (see attached), colour 32c.
Your order no. is 66193 F/2. Please refer to this number in all future correspondence.

6 **Look at the paragraphs below. Each paragraph belongs to either a formal or an informal email. Find the two emails and write the letters (a–j) below.**

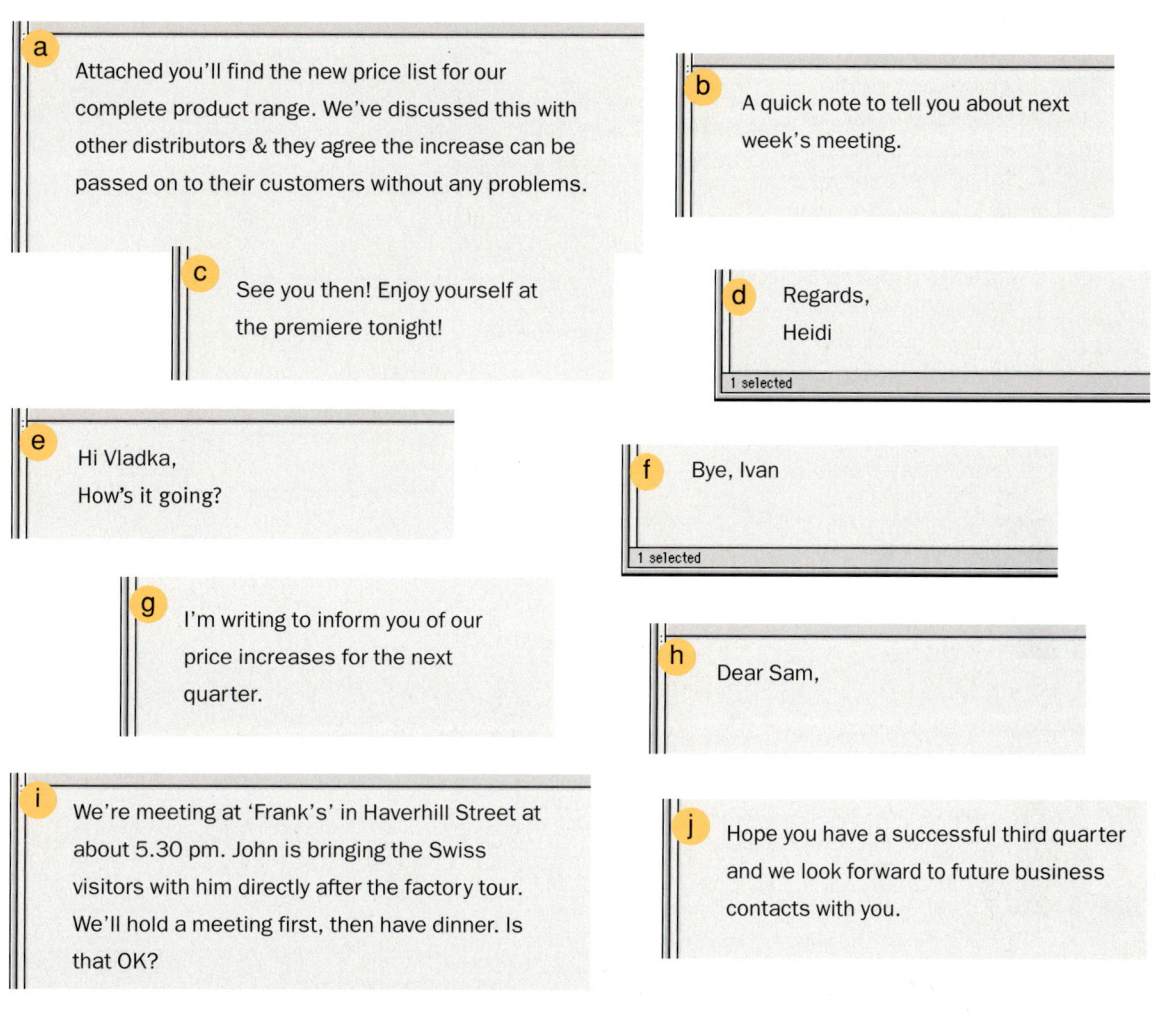

a Attached you'll find the new price list for our complete product range. We've discussed this with other distributors & they agree the increase can be passed on to their customers without any problems.

b A quick note to tell you about next week's meeting.

c See you then! Enjoy yourself at the premiere tonight!

d Regards,
Heidi

1 selected

e Hi Vladka,
How's it going?

f Bye, Ivan

1 selected

g I'm writing to inform you of our price increases for the next quarter.

h Dear Sam,

i We're meeting at 'Frank's' in Haverhill Street at about 5.30 pm. John is bringing the Swiss visitors with him directly after the factory tour. We'll hold a meeting first, then have dinner. Is that OK?

j Hope you have a successful third quarter and we look forward to future business contacts with you.

VOCABULARY ASSISTANT attached *beigefügt* distributor *Lieferant* price increase *Preiserhöhung* product range *Produktpalette* quarter *Quartal* successful *erfolgreich*

	Formal email	Informal email
salutation	☐	☐
opening sentence	☐	☐
body	☐	☐
friendly ending	☐	☐
complimentary close	☐	☐

7   **Use the clues to complete the puzzle and find the hidden word.**

1 A typical email close
2 Where messages are stored before they are sent
3 What the email is about
4 To send an email you have received to a third person: *to …*
5 The opposite of 'to send': *to …*
6 What the exclamation mark (!) stands for
7 The text of an email
8 Another word for 'answer': *Looking forward to your …*
9 Where new emails go when you first receive them
10 Part of an opening sentence: *I'm w… to let you know …*

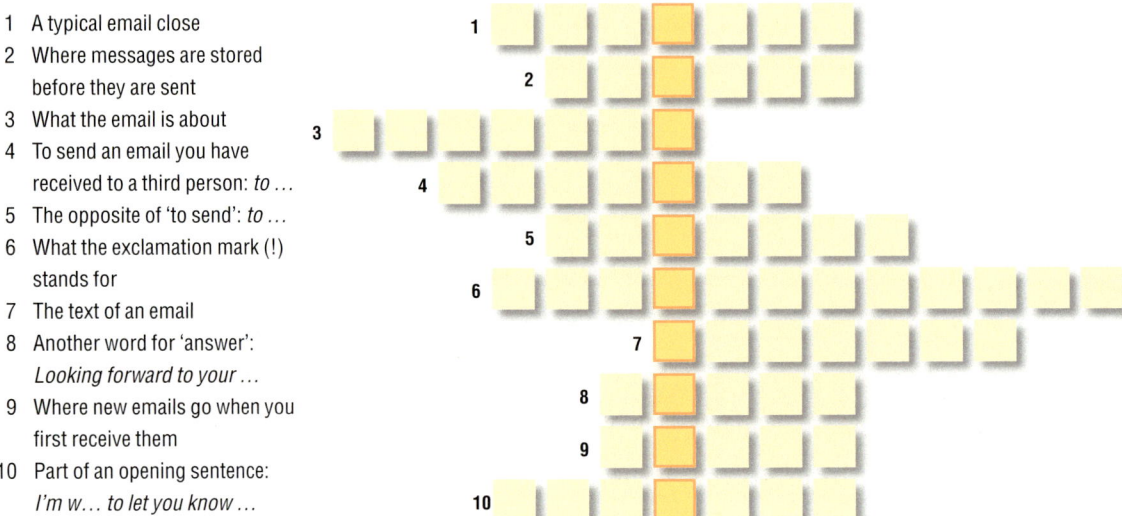

Read the article and answer the questions.

'Big brother' is watching … and checking your emails

As more and more email is used at work, firms across America are growing concerned about what their employees are saying in company emails while on company time. According to a recent survey, about 45% of firms in the USA monitor their employees' electronic communication, including email, voice mail and Internet use. And that figure is expected to rise.

For many of America's 78 million email users, this use of scanning equipment to monitor emails is too much like Orwell's 'Big Brother'. But for the companies doing the monitoring, there are many good reasons for keeping an eye on their employees.

"Inappropriate email can really damage a company in a number of ways," says Bert Taylor, a Chicago-based consultant who advises companies on security and privacy issues. "Employees can send jokes which others might see as sexual harassment. Some emails can even reveal company decisions, which can later be used by the competition or even in court."

Lost productivity isn't one of the main reasons for monitoring e-communication, but some firms are worried that workers spend too much time using computers as toys. 90% of workers say they receive personal emails during the workday.

Now many large companies are setting up policies on email and Internet use. For such policies to work, say experts, they must be in writing and they must be enforced.

Over to you
How much time a day do you spend on emails?
Does your company have an emailing policy?
Do you think companies monitor emails for security or legal reasons, or just to check on the staff?

YOU'VE GOT MAIL ▶   UNIT 1   Partner A   page 48
Partner B   page 50

Formal & informal emails

Can you show emotion in an email? Match the emoticons to the correct meaning or description.

1	:-)	a	I'm angry or shocked (shouting face)
2	:-(	b	I've just made a sweet remark (face like an angel)
3	;-)	c	I'm happy (smiley face)
4	:->	d	I'm unhappy (sad face)
5	O:-)	e	No comment (neutral face)
6	:-O	f	I've made a joke or said something funny (one eye closed)
7	:-I	g	Sarcastic comment – more powerful than ;-)

Looks like someone's having a bad day...

Now read the extracts below and add the appropriate emoticon. (More than one answer is possible.)

8 Have a nice weekend!

9 You're great! Thanks so much for helping. What would I do without you?

10 Have you heard Petra's leaving the company & moving to the competition?!

11 My computer crashed yesterday & I lost all my data!

12 I don't believe you're finally going on holiday. In fact, I didn't think you even knew what a 'holiday' was!?

13 You're going to the conference with Steve? Do you know what he's like!?

14 Sorry, I can't talk about that! Top secret!

1   Look at the emails a – f. Which messages are formal and which are informal?

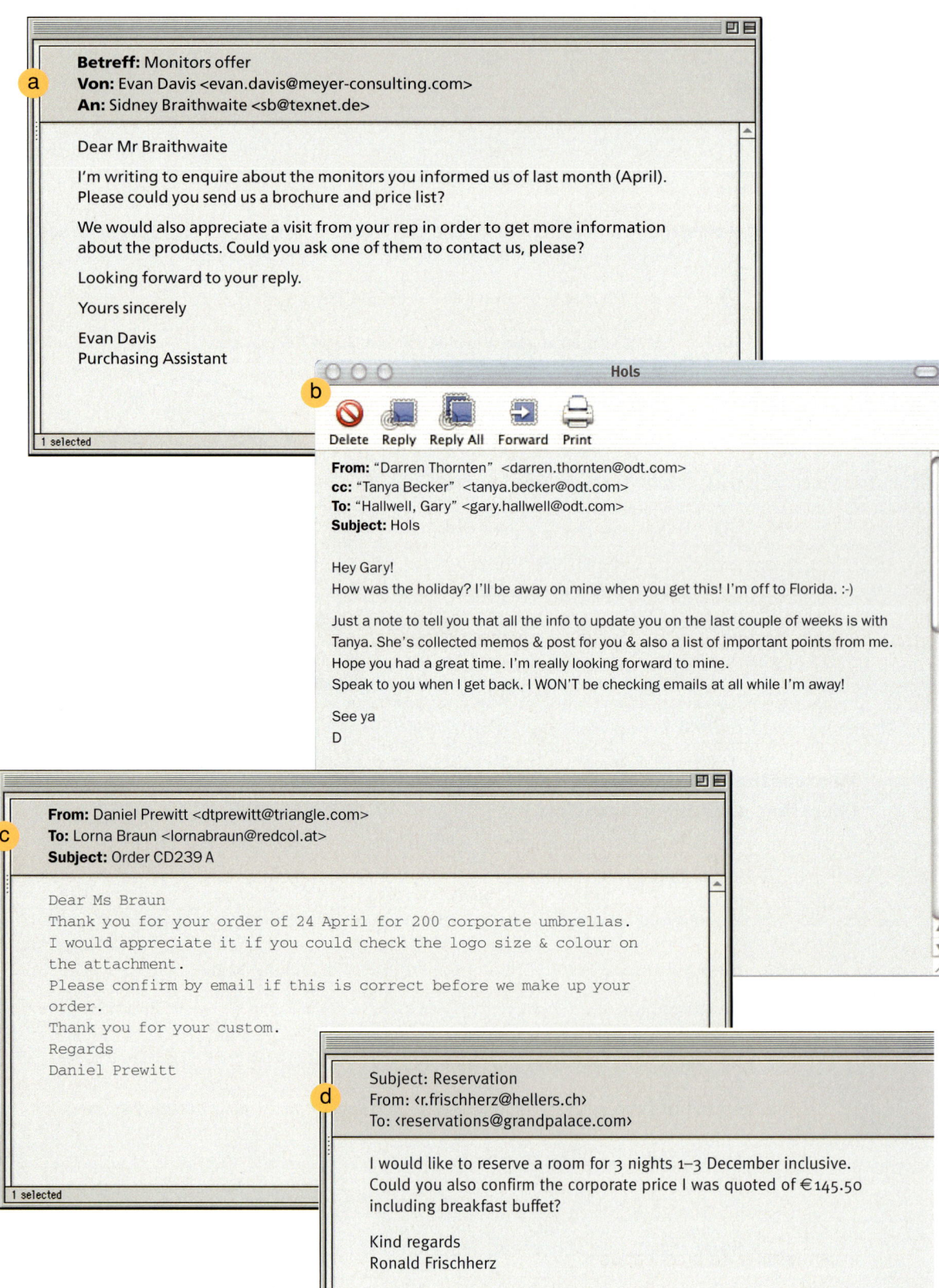

a

Betreff: Monitors offer
Von: Evan Davis <evan.davis@meyer-consulting.com>
An: Sidney Braithwaite <sb@texnet.de>

Dear Mr Braithwaite

I'm writing to enquire about the monitors you informed us of last month (April). Please could you send us a brochure and price list?

We would also appreciate a visit from your rep in order to get more information about the products. Could you ask one of them to contact us, please?

Looking forward to your reply.

Yours sincerely

Evan Davis
Purchasing Assistant

1 selected

b

Hols

Delete   Reply   Reply All   Forward   Print

From: "Darren Thornten" <darren.thornten@odt.com>
cc: "Tanya Becker" <tanya.becker@odt.com>
To: "Hallwell, Gary" <gary.hallwell@odt.com>
Subject: Hols

Hey Gary!
How was the holiday? I'll be away on mine when you get this! I'm off to Florida. :-)

Just a note to tell you that all the info to update you on the last couple of weeks is with Tanya. She's collected memos & post for you & also a list of important points from me. Hope you had a great time. I'm really looking forward to mine.
Speak to you when I get back. I WON'T be checking emails at all while I'm away!

See ya
D

c

From: Daniel Prewitt <dtprewitt@triangle.com>
To: Lorna Braun <lornabraun@redcol.at>
Subject: Order CD239 A

Dear Ms Braun
Thank you for your order of 24 April for 200 corporate umbrellas.
I would appreciate it if you could check the logo size & colour on the attachment.
Please confirm by email if this is correct before we make up your order.
Thank you for your custom.
Regards
Daniel Prewitt

1 selected

d

Subject: Reservation
From: <r.frischherz@hellers.ch>
To: <reservations@grandpalace.com>

I would like to reserve a room for 3 nights 1–3 December inclusive. Could you also confirm the corporate price I was quoted of €145.50 including breakfast buffet?

Kind regards
Ronald Frischherz

e

To: Gabriella ‹gabriella.m@bradfords.co.uk›
From: Yanis ‹yta@infotech2.co.uk›
Subject: Change of plan

Hello Gabi
I hope this email reaches you before you leave the office.
I'm afraid the rep who's coming to visit you tomorrow has been taken ill.
Would it be OK if we put off her visit until she's well?
Hope this isn't going to cause you too much trouble.
Let me know if I can be of assistance.
Have a nice day :-)
Yanis

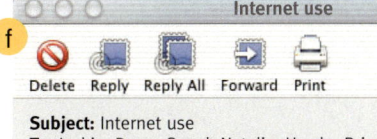

○ ○ ○　　　　　　　　　Internet use

f　⊘　　📩　　📩　　➡	🖨
　　　Delete　Reply　Reply All　Forward　Print

Subject: Internet use
To: Jackie; Dean; Sonal; Natalie; Ursula; Brian; Robert; Gerhard; Chris; Charlie; Amanda; Jane; Christian; Angela; Kati; Simon; David; Tim; Steve; Jason …
cc: Andrew Todd; Annabel Landis
From: Jenny

Dear All:
Please note that starting immediately use of the Internet during working times will be limited. Access will be granted between 15.00 – 18.00 every day.

Thank you for your cooperation.

Jenny Morris
Human Resources Assistant

VOCABULARY ASSISTANT

to appreciate *dankbar sein für*   to cause trouble *Ärger machen*   to confirm *bestätigen*
custom *Einkauf*   to enquire *erfragen*   to grant access *Zugang bewilligen*
to put off *verschieben*   to quote *Kostenvoranschlag machen*   rep (representative)
Vertreter/in   to update sb *jdm erzählen was neu ist*

2　**Now look at the emails again and find the following.**

1　An announcement to the staff of a new regulation
2　A message to a colleague
3　A message to a customer about a change in plans

4　A request for confirmation of an order
5　A hotel reservation
6　An enquiry to a supplier

 **TIP**

Register

The register of an email (how formal or informal it is) depends on the type of message you are writing and who you are writing to. Thus an email about rescheduling a meeting might be less formal than an enquiry or an apology. Similarly, an email to a new customer or the CEO of your company would probably be more formal than an email to an old customer or a colleague.

You can tell how formal an email is by its …

Salutation & close: See **TIP** on page 7.

Colloquial phrases: These are phrases normally used in conversation which make an email less formal. Examples are *How's it going?* for *How are you?* or *See ya* for *See you later.* See page 34 for more examples.

Vocabulary: The words and expressions used in an email can make it formal or informal. Some examples are:

formal	to receive	to inform	to assist	to contact
less formal	to get	to tell	to help	to get in touch

Abbreviations: The use of abbreviations and symbols (*eg* for *for example*, *info* for *information* and *&* for *and*) are more common in informal emails, although some standard abbreviations used in letter-writing – like *asap* – are also found in formal emails.

Emoticons: These written forms of body language or gesture are often used in less formal emails to help the recipient understand exactly what you mean.

3 **Find examples in the emails on pages 12 and 13 to complete the table.**

	More formal	Less formal (or informal)
saluations & closes	*Dear Mr Braithwaite*	*Hey Gary!*
phrases & vocabulary	*inform*	*Just a note to tell you …*
abbreviations, etc		*:-)*

4   **Match the vocabulary used in formal emails (1–10) with the less formal vocabulary below.**

to answer @ to ask @ to get in touch with @ help @ to need @ OK̶ @ to put off @
to be sorry @ to set up @ to tell

1   convenient   =   _OK_____   6   to contact   =   _____

2   assistance   =   _____   7   to postpone   =   _____

3   to inform   =   _____   8   to arrange   =   _____

4   to reply   =   _____   9   to enquire   =   _____

5   to regret   =   _____   10   to require   =   _____

5   **Now complete the emails below with words from above. Be careful of the register!**

---

1   Dear Mr Bass

I am writing to _____ 1 about your range of less exclusive products.

Our company has diversified recently and, in addition to the professional equipment we have previously

purchased, we now _____ 2 products for the hobby golfer.

Could we _____ 3 a meeting to see one of your sales reps who can _____ 4 us

about your products? The week of 19 August would be _____ 5 for us.

As I will be out of the office from 2 to 6 August, please _____ 6 my assistant, Sylvie Jouet,

directly.

Best regards
Simon Pilgrim

1 selected

---

2   Hi Sylvie

Just a quick note to say we are very _____ 7 for the delivery delay.

I'm afraid we'll have to _____ 8 the delivery date for 10 days because of the truck drivers' strike.

When exactly do you _____ 9 the goods? If it's very urgent I'll _____ 10 the manager

of the forwarders whether we can _____ 11 a special delivery somehow.

I'll _____ 12 asap, but please let me know the latest date for the goods.

Despite this, have a nice day!
Rgds
Jean

1 selected

VOCABULARY ASSISTANT

delay *Verspätung*   delivery *Lieferung*   despite this *trotzdem*   to diversify *diversifizieren*
forwarder *Spediteur*   goods *Waren*   previously *vorher*   to purchase *einkaufen*
range *Sortiment*   recently *vor kurzem*   urgent *dringend*

6 **What do you think the following abbreviations stand for? Write out the full meaning.**

1 ie   *in other words* _____

2 asap _____

3 Thurs _____

4 Jan _____

5 at the mo _____

6 bw _____

7 attn _____

8 rgds _____

9 pls _____

10 w/e _____

7 **Read the two emails below and find at least five things that make them either formal or informal. Then use the notes to write responses in the right register.**

Hi Johannes!

I'm coming over to Bern for a conference in 2 weeks & was wondering if you could sort out somewhere for me to stay? I've got a bit of info about the conference hotel, it's the Hotel Bern in Viktoriastrasse 43, but not sure I want to stay there! Can you help me pls?

Hope this is OK with you!

Teresa
PS How about meeting up for a drink one night? ;-)

- send map of Bern as attachment
- list of guest houses and hotels at <www.berncityscope.ch/accommodation.htm>
- dinner instead?

Dear Johannes

I'm writing to you about my visit to Bern. I'm attending a conference on 20 March and hope you can assist me in arranging accommodation. I've tried the tourist information office but they weren't very helpful.

The conference hotel is Hotel Bern in Viktoriastrasse 43 but I'd prefer to stay in a smaller guest house in the vicinity. Unfortunately I don't know Bern so it's rather difficult to find out where the best accommodation is.
I really hope the above is convenient.
Best regards
Sandy

- list of guest houses and hotels at <www.berncityscope.ch/accommodation.htm>
- can book online or should I book something?
- can recommend 'Pension Bergland' (my parents stayed there)

| **VOCABULARY ASSISTANT** | accommodation *Unterkunft* to attend *teilnehmen* to be convenient *passend / in Ordnung sein* to sort out *arrangieren* in the vicinity *in der Nähe* |

8   **Find ten spelling mistakes in the first email. Then correct the second email.**
How many mistakes can you find? (Look out for punctuation too!)

Hi Charlotta
Jsut a quik note to telll you that the info fort
he new product has finally arrived.
Ill get in tuch with you next week to update
you on tormorow#s meeting in Romania.
Can you put of the product mailing until I'm
back?
Seeyou soon.

Ragrds
Tibor

Deer Mahendra
we are still wating for the above oerder but have
recieved no email to explain the reason for the deley.
This is particularly inconvenient for us at the moment
as as our clients need the dylivery asap
Please can you kontakt the forwarders find out what
has happened and inform us immediately.
we look forward to hearing from you very soon

kind regards
Mia

How important is accuracy in emails? Which opinion do you agree with?

2 *Hmm, I'm not sure you're right! I've spoken to many native speakers and it really annoys them to receive emails with the wrong spelling and no punctuation, etc. It looks as if you don't care!*

4 *Oh, come on. I think you're overreacting a bit. Email is supposed to be quick and who has time to check spelling or grammar? I say, if the email is clear and under- standable, who cares if there are a few – or even a lot of – mistakes?*

1 *Writing emails is so easy! You don't have to worry about spelling, punctuation or the order of the information! It's great!*

3 *I agree. I get a lot of job applications sent by email and if the cover letter has too many mistakes, I don't even bother opening the attached CV. Why would I want to hire somebody who's sloppy and careless?*

5 *In my opinion, it depends on the person you're writing to. My close colleagues don't care if I make a few mistakes. But if I'm writing to someone I do business with, then I make sure my email is correct. After all, I don't want to give them the wrong impression.*

Over to you
How would you react if you received an email full of
mistakes from someone you didn't know?
Would it matter if the person wasn't writing in his
or her native language?

YOU'VE GOT MAIL   UNIT **2**   Partner A   page 48
Partner B   page 50

3 Enquiries

Can you say your email or website address?
Match each symbol with how you say it.

at @ back slash @ capital 'h' @
dot @ hyphen/dash @ slash @
small 'h' @ underscore

H	_____	**.**	_____
h	_____	**@**	_____
-	_____	**/**	_____
_	_____	****	_____

Now work with a partner. One of you look at page 51, the other look below.
Take turns dictating the email and website addresses to each other, then check your answers.

dictate		write	
1	jason.carter@gmv.de	6	_____
2	h.marlow@freeserve.com	7	_____
3	p-onigl@fib.si	8	_____
4	www.beat_top.com	9	_____
5	geoff@hmj.ch	10	_____

1 **Look at the ads below. Would you contact the companies by email, phone, fax or letter?**
What are the advantages/disadvantages of contacting the companies by email?

Net-train

Computer / Internet training

267 London Road

Norwich

Norfolk

NR35 6QY

Tel. no. 0207 5167421

Fax no. 0207 6177421

email: training@net-train.co.uk

www.net-train.co.uk

W A N T E D !

We are looking for a highly qualified receptionist
to join our team in a 5-star conference hotel.
Position available from April 1.
For further info contact: Sussie Karlsson,
Personnel Manager

Hotel Falkenberg

Box: 572

SE-31123 Falkenberg

Tel: +46 (0)346-166 50

Fax: +46 (0)346-166 58

s.karlsson@swedenhotels.se

www.hotelfalkenberg.se

All correspondence and applications
in English, please.

4 Drummond Road

Ennis

County Clare

Ireland

Tel. no. 0021 847365937

Fax no. 0021 84765852

Email request@holidays.co.ir

www.holidaysinireland.co.ir

Holidays in Ireland

2 **Look at these parts of an email requesting information about the training courses in**
the first advertisement. Connect the sentences and put them in the correct order.

1 I am interested in …
2 I look forward to …
3 Could you please send me …
4 I saw your advert in …

a … information on the length, cost and contents?
b … the Financial Times of 5 January.
c … hearing from you soon.
d … your Internet training courses.

Use similar phrases to write a short request to advertisement 2 or 3.

3   **Complete the table with the phrases below.**

Can you help? @ We hope you are happy with this. @ Let us know if you need any more help. @
Please answer asap. @ I'm sending you the ... in an attachment. @ I'm sending you ... @
Thanks for choosing ... @ We are working on your request. @ Can you please send me ... ? @
Thanks for your email/request.

More formal	Less formal	
Requesting information		
Could you please send me ... ?	_____	1
Would you be able to help ... ?	_____	2
I'd appreciate a reply asap.	_____	3
Replies		
Thank you for your email/enquiry.	_____	4
I'm pleased to send you ...	_____	5
Please find the ... in an attachment.	_____	6
Your request is being processed.	_____	7
We hope you find this satisfactory.	_____	8
Thank you for your interest.	_____	9
Do not hesitate to contact us if you require further assistance.	_____	10

4   **Use (parts of) the phrases in exercise 3 to complete the request and reply emails below.**

From: rachel.beamish@wells.co.uk   **To:** request@changingrooms.co.uk
Subject: Request for brochures
_____

Our company is currently looking for accommodation for some
overseas colleagues who will be transferred to Southampton for
12 months.

_____¹ me some brochures showing the
various houses and flats you have to offer. We also need to find
locations near schools; _____²?
As our employees are arriving next month, I _____
_____³.
Thank you very much.

Best regards
Rachel Beamish
HR assistant
Wells Ltd

Subject: Re. Request for brochures
To: rachel.beamish@wells.co.uk

From: Brian Pearson ‹Brian@changingrooms.co.uk›
Attachment: Southampton.pdf

Dear Ms Beamish

_____ [4]. Unfortunately, the brochure you requested is being

reprinted at the moment, but _____ [5]. Prices and location have

remained the same, however, so you'll find the requested information _____

_____ [6]. The new brochure will be sent by post as soon as it's available.

We _____ [7].

_____ [8].

Regards

Brian Pearson
Relocation Specialist
Changing Rooms
Brian@changingrooms.co.uk
www.changingrooms.co.uk

 **VOCABULARY ASSISTANT**   available *verfügbar*   currently *zurzeit*   employee *Mitarbeiter/in*   however *jedoch, aber*   location *Lage*   to be transferred *versetzt werden*   unfortunately *leider*

➡ **TIP**   **Polite language**

Even in informal emails, it is important to use polite language.
Please can be used in every type of request, and phrases with ***could*** and ***would like*** are more polite than phrases with ***can*** or ***want***.

> *Could you please send me …*
> *I would like to order …*

> *Can you please send me …*
> *I want to order …*

In enquiries it is best to avoid imperatives like 'Send me …' or 'Inform me …'. By adding ***please*** the sentence becomes more polite, but is still rather direct.

> *Please send me your current price list …*
> *Please give us your rates …*

The following phrases can be used in formal enquiries to first-time contacts. However, they can sound too formal in emails to colleagues.

> *We would be grateful if you could send us …*
> *We would also appreciate some information on …*

5   **Rewrite these emails to make them polite.**

> Our general manager saw your advert in yesterday's Financial Times and wants
> the free start-up packet advertised.
> Send it to:
> …
> We also want all the information you can send us on your after-sales service.
> Thanks in advance.
> T. Gerald

> Dear Giovanni
> Jane at headquarters gave me your name and said you will help me. I need some
> information about the upcoming trade fair in Milan.
> 1) Who is attending from the Milan office?
> 2) How many hotel rooms have you booked?
> 3) What time and where is the Tuesday night reception?
> Send me the information immediately.
> Regards
> Martin
> PS   I want you to send me your extension number too. I can't find it on the
> international list.

6   **Unscramble the words below, then use them to complete the gaps.**
   (Tip: the first letter of the word is always correct!)

apsa @ arppctieae @ antttmahce @ eqyuirn @ iertentsed @ kwon @ rqtseue @
rvceiee @ snde @ stfcrisaatoy

1   I'm sending you the price list in the

     _attachment_____ .

2   Your _____ is being processed.

3   Please answer _____ .

4   We hope you find this _____ .

5   Can you _____ me … ?

6   I'd _____ a reply asap.

7   Thank you for your _____ .

8   Let me _____ if you need any
     more help.

9   I'm _____ in … .

10   I would like to _____ … .

7   **Use the information below to write an enquiry.**

You are the sales rep for Bigtop electric drills and saws in Saxony.
Write to James Baker (Ute Müller gave you his name) to order some brochures on Bigtop's after-sales
service. You need the English version of the brochures for a trade fair in the Czech Republic.
The trade fair is next week!

8   **You receive the two enquiries below. Use your notes to write the replies.**

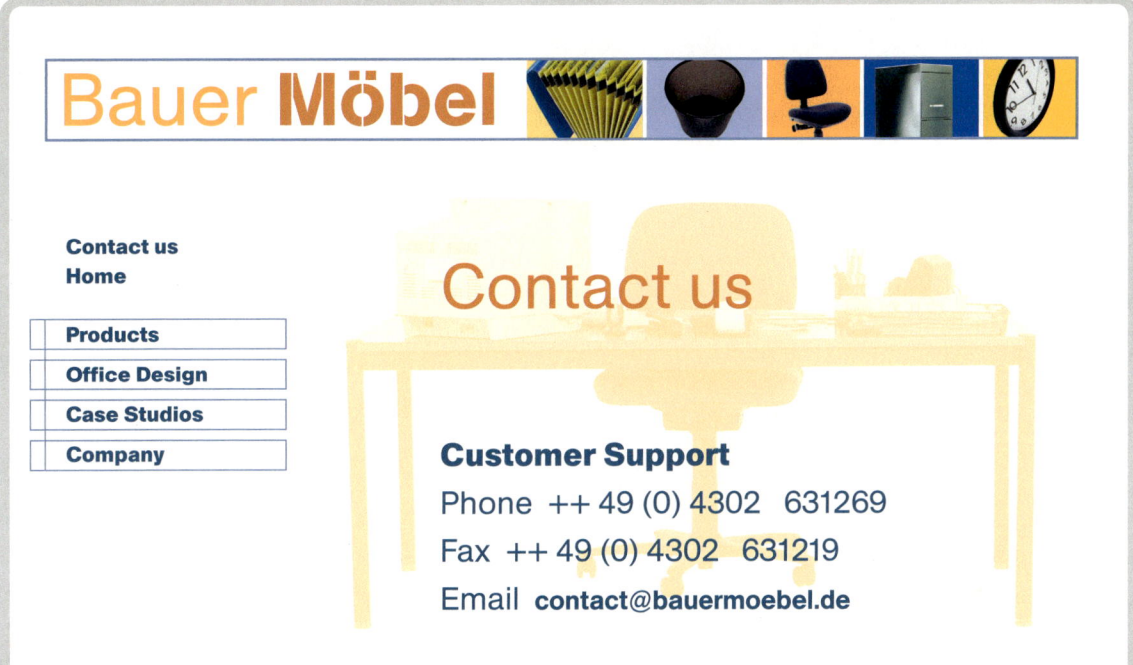

Bauer Möbel

Contact us
Home

| **Products** |
| **Office Design** |
| **Case Studios** |
| **Company** |

Contact us

Customer Support

Phone ++ 49 (0) 4302 631269

Fax ++ 49 (0) 4302 631219

Email **contact@bauermoebel.de**

To: contact@bauermoebel.de
From: pia@vml.nl
Re: office furniture 'progress'

We are a medium-sized engineering company in Amsterdam and are interested in your range of office furniture 'progress'.
Could you please send us a catalogue and a current price list?
As we are in the process of deciding on office furniture for our new building, I'd appreciate a prompt reply.

Thank you for your help.

Pia Stevens

V.M.L. BV
Keizersgracht 384
Amsterdam 1016GB
Netherlands
Tel: +31 20 5 30 20 10
Fax: +31 20 5 30 20 30
e-mail: pia@vml.nl
website: www.vml.nl

package sent this morning, also attached as PDF file

To: contact@bauermoebel.de
From: sandy.adams1@web.de
Re: info

Hello
I saw your website and would like to know where I can find your furniture in the Hamburg area.
Also, can you please send me a catalogue?
My address is
Sandy Adams
Königstrasse 15
22869 Schenefeld

Thanks!
S. Adams

list attached with shops and addresses

catalogue sent by post this morning

OUTBOX

Read and discuss the article.

The Danger of Viruses

Scenario 1

You receive an email from an unknown company. Nothing unusual about that? You receive enquiries everyday. But this one has the subject line: I LOVE YOU. What do you do?

Scenario 2

You receive an email from a friend you haven't heard from in years and see it includes a very short impersonal message and an attachment. Do you open the attachment or delete it?

Warnings of viruses – whether forwarded by friends or announced over the radio – have now become so common, it's difficult to know whether or not to take them seriously. Most companies play it safe and install so-called 'firewalls' which screen emails as they enter the system and prevent suspicious programs from infecting the computer network. You can also buy virus detection software, which can be updated from the Internet to protect PCs from viruses. However neither of these precautions is 100% safe.

The best advice is to be aware of viruses and to check emails carefully before opening them. If the email has no sender name, or contains attachments from people you don't know, it's best not to open them. Often viruses are unknowingly passed on, so you may receive an email from a colleague, but it has an unrelated attachment or an attachment with a strange name. In these cases, it's best to contact your colleague and ask what the attachment is before opening it.

Computer viruses aren't a new phenomena: in 1988 the 'Morris worm' virus infected nearly 10% of computers which had access to the Internet. Nowadays viruses are getting more sophisticated, though, so if your PC is used for emailing, it's best to be very careful and not open anything that looks suspicious.

Over to you

Has your computer ever had a virus? Tell your colleague what happened.

What steps does your company take to protect against viruses?

There are people who think some 'viruses' are hoaxes, spread by companies who sell virus protection. (See, for example, http://vmyths.com) Do you agree?

YOU'VE GOT MAIL ▶ UNIT 3 | Partner A   page 48 / Partner B   page 50

4 Requesting action

Emails – especially those from native speakers of English – can contain a lot of acronyms and abbreviations. How many do you know? If you have trouble finding the answers, look at the clues below.

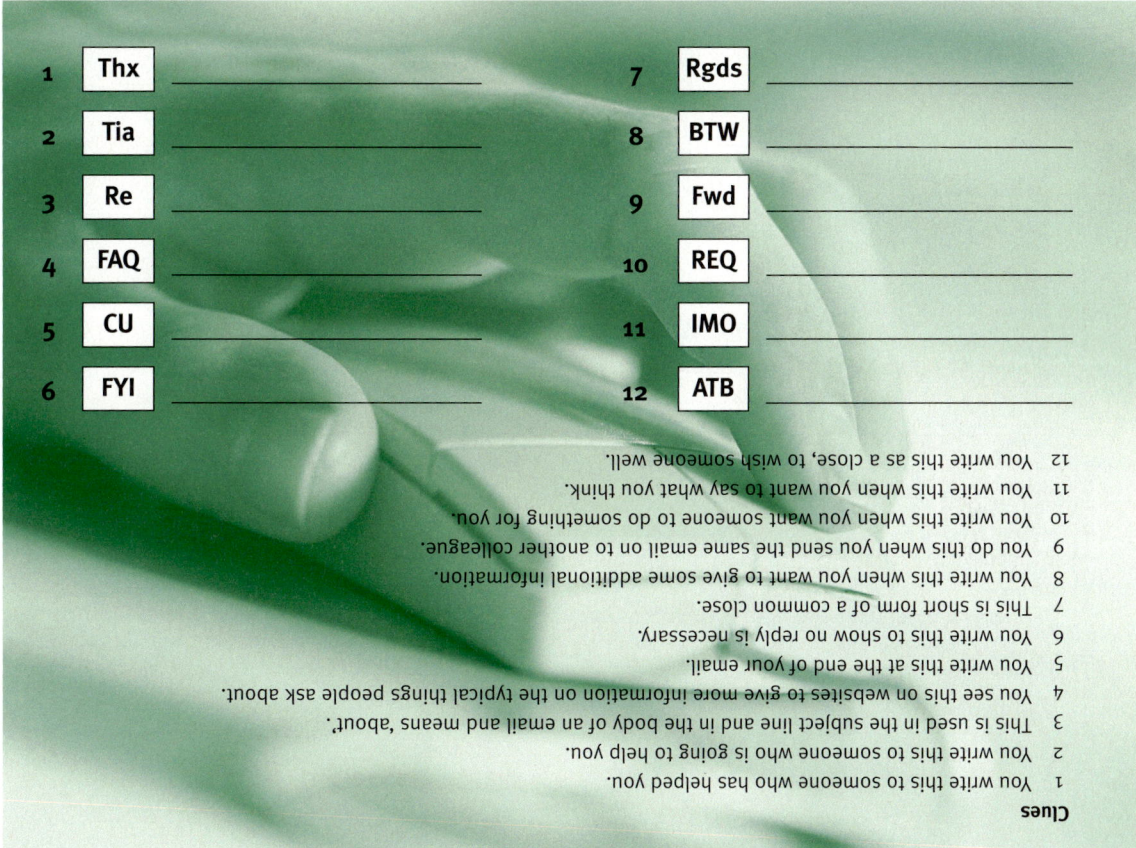

1	Thx	_____
2	Tia	_____
3	Re	_____
4	FAQ	_____
5	CU	_____
6	FYI	_____

7	Rgds	_____
8	BTW	_____
9	Fwd	_____
10	REQ	_____
11	IMO	_____
12	ATB	_____

Clues

1 You write this to someone who has helped you.
2 You write this to someone who is going to help you.
3 This is used in the subject line and in the body of an email and means 'about'.
4 You see this on websites to give more information on the typical things people ask about.
5 You write this at the end of your email.
6 You write this to show no reply is necessary.
7 This is short form of a common close.
8 You write this when you want to give some additional information.
9 You do this when you send the same email on to another colleague.
10 You write this when you want someone to do something for you.
11 You write this when you want to say what you think.
12 You write this as a close, to wish someone well.

The use of abbreviations and acronyms is not the only way native speakers try to keep their messages short. They often also omit articles, pronouns or auxiliary verbs. Look at these sentences and write them out in full.

1 Looking fwd to seeing u next wk.
2 Tia for yr help.
3 Will be in touch tomorrow with updated figures.
4 Pls call me re our meeting on Thurs am.

5 Just a quick email to give you new dates.
6 Got any exciting plans for the w/e?
7 No info on pay rises at the mo. Hope to hear sth soon though.

1   Read the two emails below and answer the questions.

1   What tasks would Simon like Pascal, Barbara and Thilo to do?
2   Which tasks have been completed and by whom? What problem has this person had?
3   What do you think the working relationship is between the four colleagues?

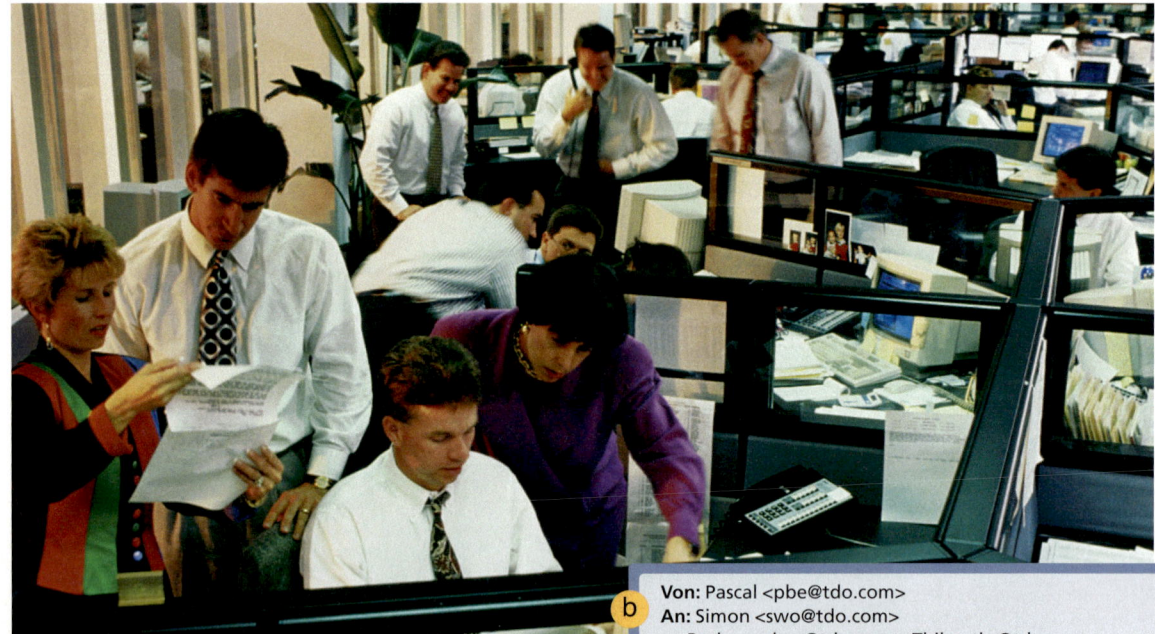

a

Von: Simon <swo@tdo.com>
An: Pascal <pbe@tdo.com>, Barbara <baz@tdo.com>, Thilo <thr@tdo.com>
Betreff: quarterly sales reports

Hi all
I'd like you to send me the figures from the last quarter by tomorrow morning first thing. Pls let me know if you have a problem with this deadline.

Pascal: Have you coordinated your team & their results yet? Can you send the report to me by Thurs 4th?

Babs: Have you finished your sales report yet? By Tues 2nd June pls.

Thilo: Have you contacted Hungary about the new account details? Gerry needs this info asap.

Please reply asap.
Best wishes
Simon

1 selected

b

Von: Pascal <pbe@tdo.com>
An: Simon <swo@tdo.com>
cc: Barbara <baz@tdo.com>, Thilo <thr@tdo.com>
Betreff: re quarterly sales report

Anlage: sales_div2_1quart.xls

Simon
I'm sending you all the info you need for last quarter in the attachment.

I've already contacted my team and they have just finished their sales figures. Unfortunately we haven't completed the report yet as we've been very busy with trade fair prep.

The deadline should be no problem though: you'll have it on your desk by 4 May.

Rgds
Pascal

VOCABULARY ASSISTANT   account *Kunde*   deadline *Frist*   delivery *Lieferung*   figures *Zahlen*   first thing *früh am Morgen*   quarterly *viertel jährlich*   report *Bericht*

 **TIP**   **Talking about deadlines and taking action**

The present perfect is used to talk about deadlines and whether or not they have been met. It is also used to describe the status of tasks in progress.

> *Have you **coordinated** your team & their results yet?*
> *I**'ve** already **contacted** my team and they **have** just **finished** their sales figures.*

Adverbs like *yet*, *already* or *just* are often used with the present perfect in this type of sentence.

> *Have you sent in your registration for the conference **yet** (= schon)?*
> *Sorry, I have**n't** written the report **yet** (= noch nicht).*
> *I've **already** (= schon) sent the registration form.*
> *We've **just** (= gerade) received the order.*

In the USA the simple past is used instead of the present perfect with the signal words above. There is no difference in meaning.

> *Did you send in your registration **yet**?*

The will future is used in replies to emails requesting action to say what the writer will do and when. Note that the contracted form (*'ll* instead of *will*) is usually used.

> *You**'ll have** it on your desk by 4 May.*
> *Sorry, but I haven't sent it yet. I**'ll do** it straight away.*

2   **A virus has infected Simon's computer and scrambled Barbara's and Thilo's replies to Simon's email. Unscramble the sentences and put them in the correct order. (Tip: the words in bold stay where they are.)**

Barbara's reply
a **Things** so here been busy have **that** hasn't on it there work been time to.
b **Last** desk a.m. figures will tomorrow your on quarters' be.
c **Tuesday** though be problem should no.
d **Sorry, Simon,** report yet finished I the haven't but.

Thilo's reply
e **I've also** that the figures wanted you attached.
f **I've** the post copy put a already in **but** an too sending as attachment am it.
g **Simon, Anna** just the at account details has the sent Hungarian office.

3 **Use the words in brackets to complete the gaps in these emails.**

Hello Jane

First of all, there _____ [1] (be) a meeting next Thursday from 2 to 5 pm to discuss trade fair planning. Please let me know whether you can attend.

_____ the brochures for model 564Z and 566T _____ [2] (you/order/yet)? Remember, we need 5000 copies each for the trade fair.

_____ Margot about the schedule _____ [3] (you/contact/yet)? I need the finalized version for the meeting on Thursday.

Finally, _____ the presentation material _____ [4] (you/send/yet)? I can't seem to find it anywhere.

Ramon

Hi Ramon

Yes, I can attend the meeting next Thursday.

I _____ [5] (just/order) the brochures for both models. They _____ [6] (be delivered) on 7 September. BTW, I _____ [7] (just/have a look) at a pdf of the new brochure. It looks good. _____ [8] (you/see) it? If not, I _____ [9] (forward) it to you.

Re the schedule: I _____ [10] (leave) a message on Margot's voicemail but she _____ [11] (call back/yet). I _____ [12] (try) again later and _____ [13] (ask) her to contact you directly.

I _____ [14] (email) the presentation material straight away. Sorry for the delay.

ATB
Jane

4 **Use words from the two lists to make as many verb-noun phrases as you can.**

Example: *to arrange an appointment or a meeting*

arrange @ attach @ clarify @ demand @ finalize @ inform @ meet @ notify @ schedule @ send @ update @ write	an appointment @ colleagues @ a database @ a deadline @ details @ a document @ a meeting @ the minutes @ payment @ a report

Then complete the sentences with words from the boxes.

1 I'm _____ you the report by post. Can you please read it and give me your feedback?

2 Please _____ your colleagues that our monthly meeting has been changed to Wednesday.

3 I've _____ an appointment with the new sales rep.

4 Clara, I've read your notes but can we meet to _____ the details.

5 I'm afraid we won't be able to meet the _____ . We're going to need a few more weeks.

6 Please email me your notes from the last meeting so that John can _____ the minutes.

7 I also need your January figures so that we can _____ the database.

8 Motor Supply Ltd still hasn't paid. It's time to demand _____ with an official letter.

5 **Look at this informal reply to an email. What questions or requests did Annika write in the original email?**

To: Annika Fornakova <ako@tagumwelt.de>
From: Martin Ho <mho@tagumwelt.de>
Subject: re Internet guidelines
Attachment: internetguidelines.doc; internetaccess.xcl

Hi Annika

How are you? Thanks for your mail.

1 Could you send me a copy of the new Internet guidelines, please?

Yes, you can have a copy of the new Internet guidelines. I haven't sent them yet as they only arrived this morning! You'll find a copy attached.

2

You also asked for my thoughts about the guidelines – no comment! :-/

3

I've also attached the stats showing Internet use in the company – just as you asked.

4

I haven't heard from Sanji for ages either but I think she's been on holiday. Perhaps Ian knows.

You asked if I have the dates of the next internal policies meeting – yes, but I'll have to find them first! ;-) Will send them asap!

Look forward to your next mail.
Have a good weekend!

5

Martin

Now write the original request in full.

6   **Your boss has given you this 'to do' list before leaving on a business trip.**
You've ticked (✔) the jobs which have been done and added some notes.
Use the 'to do' list to answer your boss's email.

- phone suppliers about our credit period ✔
  extension of 30 days

              not available on days we need!
- book room at ~~Hilton~~ for Japanese guests – want to hold reception,
  10 participants approx
          booked room at International

                        International
- get an offer for buffet lunch from ~~Hilton~~ ✔ *EUR 50 a person*

- check my parking permit has been renewed *can leave till end of week*

- organize times for in-company language training –
  NOT in core-time! ✔

- correct my overheads for Thursday presentation

- phone Jeff – cancel golf morning for Friday *left message on mailbox,*
                                          will try again

- ask Tessa to call me next Tues re: travel expenses ✔

Delete Reply Reply All Forward Print

The presentation went well, but we've come to a standstill
on terms and conditions. This means I'll have to stay another
2 days.
Could you please call Steve and ask him if he can do my
presentation on Thursday for me?
Could you also update me by tomorrow evening on what you've
done from that list? I'll have a bit of time tomorrow to go through
my emails and do some work on my laptop.
Hope you have a nice evening – don't work too hard!
Roger

To cc or not to cc? Which opinion(s) do you agree with?

Carla: I get over 160 emails a day and most of them are totally useless. Just copies of emails to other colleagues, replies to those emails, comments on the replies, etc, etc. And most of the information has nothing to do with me. So, what's the point?

Samuel: I see your point but you shouldn't forget that a lot of decisions are made by email now. Things that used to be put in writing – and by that I mean official memos or formal letters sent by post – are now just being confirmed and recorded electronically. How many people do you know who actually print out their important emails so there's a hard copy? If I didn't get copies electronically, I wouldn't know what's happening.

Joan: I agree. I also get lots of emails where I've just been copied in. Maybe my colleagues are being nice to want to include me and not leave me out of the loop. But, let's face it, most of the time I don't really need the information. And especially in a long email exchange between two colleagues, wouldn't it be more effective for them to just send me (and the ten other people on the cc list) the results once they've finished their discussion?

Larry: My boss insists on getting blind copies of everything. And I'm supposed to cc everyone in my team. I guess she wants to make sure that we all have the same knowledge and that nobody is left out. But it means I spend a lot of time reading through emails.

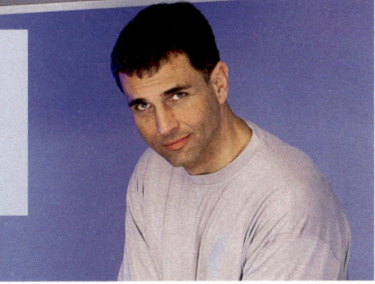

Tad: Hey, I don't know what you're all complaining about! I wish someone would cc me now and then! Nobody ever sends me copies of anything, even when the emails are about something I should know for my work. I wish this function were used more in our company.

Over to you

How often do you use the cc function and who do you send copies to?
Do you ever use the blind copy (bcc) function?
Does your company – or team – have a policy
on who is copied in?

YOU'VE GOT MAIL ➤ **UNIT 4**   Partner A page 49
Partner B page 50

Exchanging information

INBOX

How has email affected our business lives and relationships? Do this quiz and check your answers below. Then discuss the answers with a colleague.

1 The average number of emails an office worker receives per day in the UK is:
- a 25
- b 85
- c 190

2 Nielsen/NetRatings track trends in Internet use. Their research showed that, in August 2002, the number of people logging onto the Internet while at work was:
- a 10 million
- b 25.3 million
- c 30.8 million

3 According to a recent survey, what percentage of greeting cards are sent electronically?
- a 5%
- b 27%
- c 79%

4 From the same survey, 16% of the 18–24-year-olds questioned sign their emails 'with love and kisses' to
- a their boyfriend/girlfriend?
- b their parents/relatives?
- c their boss?

5 There are now three times more corporate (electronic) mail boxes in America than five years ago. How many do you think there are?
- a 1 million
- b 170 million
- c 1 billion

6 What percentage of the population of the USA use email at home or work?
- a 40%
- b 75%
- c 100%

7 The majority of the online population have English as their native language (40.2%). Which language comes next?
- a Spanish
- b Korean
- c Chinese

8 What percentage of all online users have German as their native language?
- a 3.2%
- b 6.6%
- c 15.4%

KEY

1c 190 on average – five fewer than in the USA. (source: survey by Pitney Bowes communications specialists)
2b 25.3 million
3b 27% according to a survey of 2000 adults carried out by ICM Research in January 2001.
4c Their boss! (source: see above) Younger people are finding the formal/informal language split less important.
5b 170 million, according to Eric Arrum from 'Messaging Online'. The survey was done in 2000 so it's estimated the figure could have nearly doubled in 2002!
6a 40% – remember that a large section of the population is either retired or pre-school, but this 40% is still almost half the population! (source Global Reach Sept 2002 – global-reach.biz/globstats)
7c Chinese makes up 10.8 % of online users, Spanish 7.4% and Korean only 4.5%. (See source above.)
8b 6.6 % – this figure is relatively high because people in German-speaking countries are highly developed with regards to technology. (See source above.)

1 **David and Mike both work for a distribution company dealing in mobile phones.**
Look at David's email and answer the questions.

1 How does Mike introduce the subject of the email?
2 Label parts of the email with the following: salutation, informing, stating the action to be taken, giving a deadline, close.
3 Does David already know about the invoice? How do you know?
4 What is the new information Mike has found out?
5 What does Mike ask David to do?

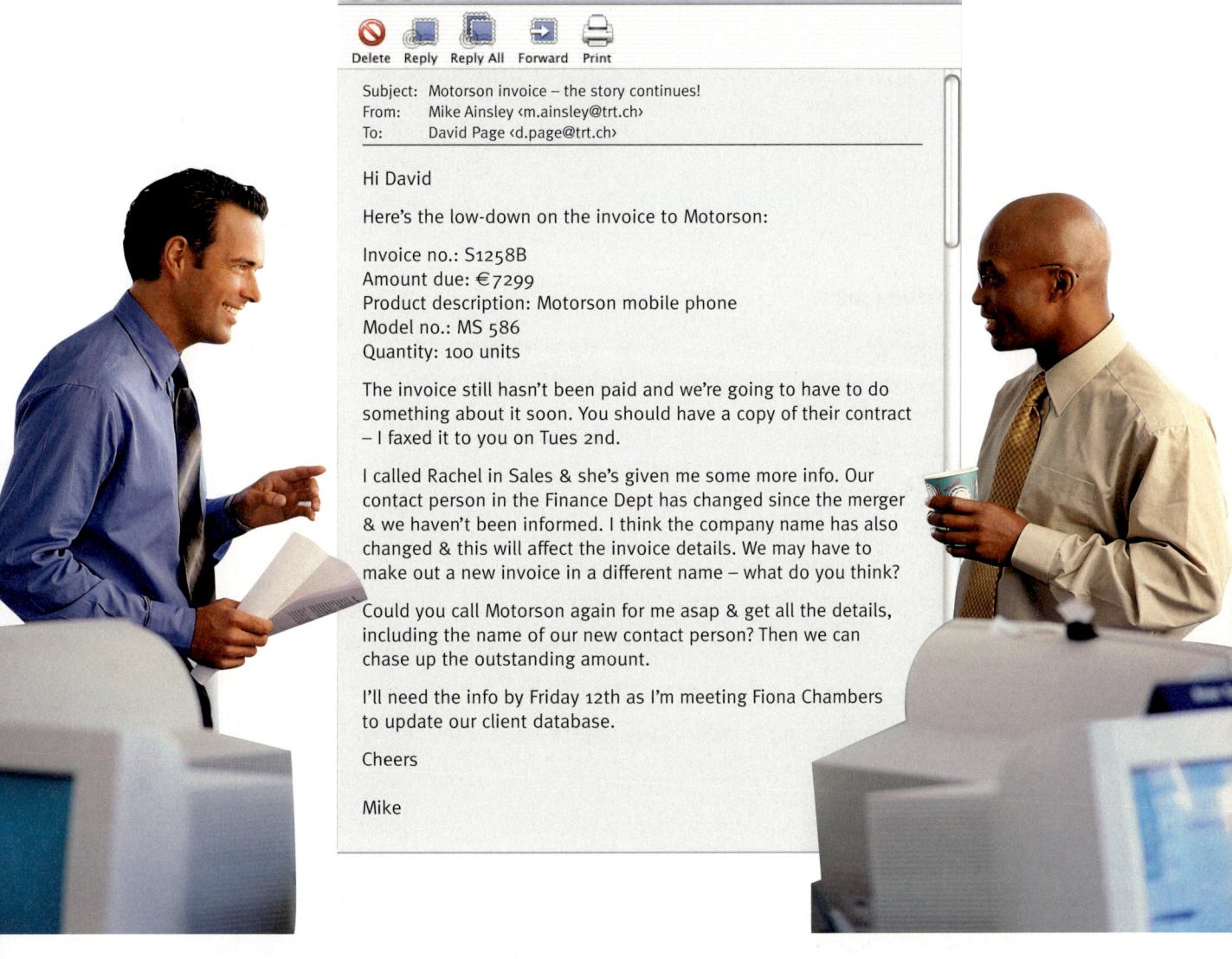

Delete Reply Reply All Forward Print

Subject: Motorson invoice – the story continues!
From: Mike Ainsley <m.ainsley@trt.ch>
To: David Page <d.page@trt.ch>

Hi David

Here's the low-down on the invoice to Motorson:

Invoice no.: S1258B
Amount due: €7299
Product description: Motorson mobile phone
Model no.: MS 586
Quantity: 100 units

The invoice still hasn't been paid and we're going to have to do something about it soon. You should have a copy of their contract – I faxed it to you on Tues 2nd.

I called Rachel in Sales & she's given me some more info. Our contact person in the Finance Dept has changed since the merger & we haven't been informed. I think the company name has also changed & this will affect the invoice details. We may have to make out a new invoice in a different name – what do you think?

Could you call Motorson again for me asap & get all the details, including the name of our new contact person? Then we can chase up the outstanding amount.

I'll need the info by Friday 12th as I'm meeting Fiona Chambers to update our client database.

Cheers

Mike

VOCABULARY ASSISTANT

amount due *ausstehender Betrag* to chase sth up (AE down) *einer Sache nachgehen* the low-down *die (wichtigsten) Informationen* to make out an invoice *eine Rechnung erstellen* merger *Fusion* outstanding amount *ausstehende Summe*

 **TIP** **Colloquial phrases and contractions**

Colloquial phrases

When English native speakers write to each other as close business acquaintances they often use colloquial phrases like *the low-down*, *to chase something up* (AE *down*) or *cheers* (BE for *thanks*). Be careful when using colloquial phrases as they can make your English sound too familiar when used in the wrong context.

Contractions

Emails often have the quality of spoken English and tend to use contractions instead of the full form, eg *here's* (*here is*), *haven't* (*have not*) or *I'll* (*I will*).

Watch out: don't leave out the apostrophe when using contractions as the meaning could be changed.

it's = *es/sie/er ist*   its = *sein/ihr*   I'll = *ich werde*   ill = *krank*

2 **Find the matching pairs.**

colloquial language	standard language
1 to check sth out	to send sb an email
2 to touch base with sb	to give sb information
3 to send sth by snail mail	to send sth by post
4 to mail* sb	to try to find or get sth (that is missing)
5 to give sb the low-down	to look at sth in detail
6 to chase sth up (AE: down)	to get in contact with sb
7 to be out of the loop	to postpone sth (or put sth off)
8 to put sth on hold	to be out of touch or not have heard sth

* Watch out when 'mail' is used as a verb; in AE *to mail* also means sending something by the traditional postal service (ie *by snail mail*)!

Now rewrite this email using standard language to replace the colloquial phrases.

Hello Uta
Thanks for getting in touch and giving me the low-down on the March sales meeting. By the way, I called Birgit's office and tried to chase up the January figures but she's been on holiday – so no success there! Perhaps you could touch base with Gerd and ask him to mail me the info directly. I hope he can – I'd hate to have to put the meeting on hold. Oh, one last thing: can you send me a few of the new brochures? No hurry – snail mail will do!
Ciao
Jon

1 selected

3   **A virus has knocked out all the apostrophes in these sentences. Put them back in.**

1   The employees were asked to comment on a no-smoking policy. Well report the results in our next online bulletin.
2   Were happy the negotiations ended positively for both parties.
3   Lets introduce Internet access for all of our employees. Theyve been using it for years anyway.
4   The production plants just had its yearly safety examination and no problems have been reported.
5   If you havent received the report, let me know & Ill send it on.
6   Heres the survey. Remember, well have to scrap the product if its not popular.

4   **David has replied to Mike's email in exercise 1 by 'quoting' from the original message. Complete David's email with items a–e.**

a   No problem. According to their message, they're back on the 9th. I'll get back to you with the info asap.
b   Thanks for yr email. I've written my answers in below.
c   I agree. Let's discuss it with the new contact person though.
d   Yes, I got it. Thanks.
e   I've tried to call but the answerphone picks up. Apparently they're all on holiday! ;-) I'll keep trying though.

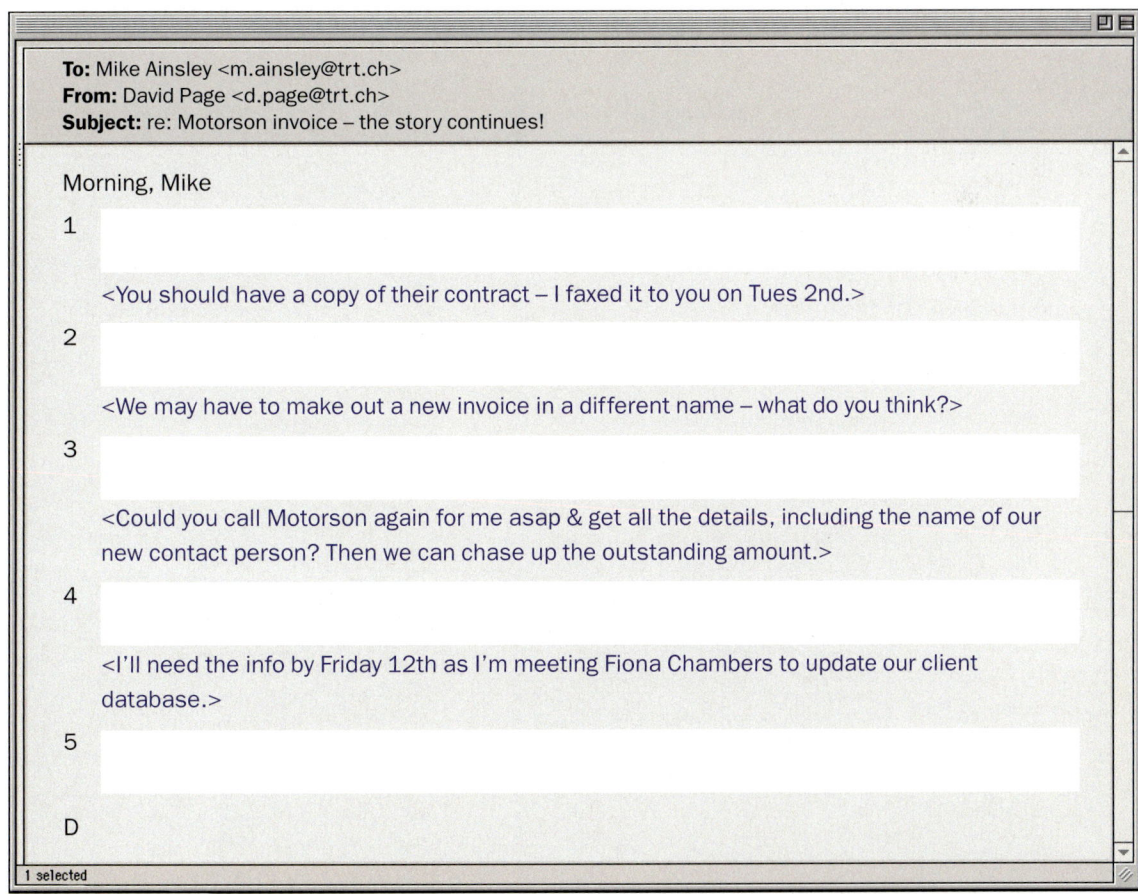

To: Mike Ainsley <m.ainsley@trt.ch>
From: David Page <d.page@trt.ch>
Subject: re: Motorson invoice – the story continues!

Morning, Mike

1

    <You should have a copy of their contract – I faxed it to you on Tues 2nd.>

2

    <We may have to make out a new invoice in a different name – what do you think?>

3

    <Could you call Motorson again for me asap & get all the details, including the name of our new contact person? Then we can chase up the outstanding amount.>

4

    <I'll need the info by Friday 12th as I'm meeting Fiona Chambers to update our client database.>

5

D

1 selected

5 **Put the following phrases in the correct category, informing or replying.**

Just a note to say/tell you ... @ In reply to your email ... @ Here are the details on ... @
I'm writing to clarify ... @ I'll get back to you asap ... @ Thank you for clarifying ... @
I'll follow up the points mentioned in your email ... @ I'd like to inform you of ... @
Just a few comments about/on ... @ Just to update you on ... @ Let me fill you in on ... @
Thanks for your email. @ You'll find the info attached ...

Informing	Replying
Just a note to say/tell you ...	*In reply to your email ...*
_____	_____
_____	_____
_____	_____
_____	_____
_____	_____
_____	_____

6 **Use (parts of) the phrases in exercise 5 to complete these short emails.**
More than one answer may be possible.

1

From: Monica Jason   **To:** Janice Forbes
Subject: Market research _____

Hey Janice!
Just _____[1] the market
research idea. We've 2000 participants & the start-up
date is Oct 1. The rest of the details aren't clear so I'll
_____[2].

Best wishes
Monica :-)

2

From: David Collins   **To:** Alison Price
Subject: Special Offer

Dear Ms Price
I'd _____[3] a special offer
we're giving to all our most loyal customers. For any
order of office supplies which exceeds €200 we shall
include a free stationery kit. For more details of this
offer you'll find _____[4].

Regards

David Collins
Customer Services

3

From: Phoebe Marlow   **To:** Gerald Ainsley
Subject: re: Updates _____

Dear Gerald
In _____[5]: I've put together
all the answers to your questions in a Word document
which I can either fax you or send as an attachment.
Which would you prefer?

Speak to you soon

Phoebe

4

From: Steve East   **To:** Timothy Barker
Subject: re: conference info – again!!

Hi Tim
Thanks _____[6]. It sounds as
if you still haven't got that info about the conference.
Let _____[7] the important
details. (I'll also post the packet to you.) It's taking
place on Wed and Thurs 25–26.8. at the Adele
Conference Centre in York and we're starting each day
at 9 am. Your presentation is on Wed at 2 pm – you've
only got 40 minutes so talk fast!

Bye for now
Steve

 **TIP**   **Being diplomatic**

When things aren't going according to plan, an email exchange can become heated. The use of diplomatic language lets you point out mistakes gently, without offending the person you're writing to.

> We have a **slight / minor / little** problem.
> **Unfortunately,** the mistake is **rather** serious.
> **I'm afraid** we're not happy with …

Furthermore, be careful when showing emotion in an email. Using exclamation marks and writing words or phrases in capital letters can make your message too strong – it can look like you're shouting.

> Joanne, I'm still waiting for a reply!!!
> Didn't we agree to meet on TUESDAY?

A more moderate way to emphasize a word is to enclose it in asterisks.

> Just writing to see what happened to your report. I needed it *Monday* and it's now Friday. Can we discuss?

7   **Rewrite the following email to make it more diplomatic.**

Helen
We have a problem! I asked you to send me the conference details LAST WEEK but I still haven't received anything. What's going on?!! Now the hotel has asked me for the info today or we will lose the reservation. This is NOT a good situation!!! This is the ONLY hotel available in Madstown for our dates and I don't want to have to change the conference location.
PLEASE TAKE CARE OF THIS IMMEDIATELY!
Jack

8   **Use these notes to write emails to some colleagues.**

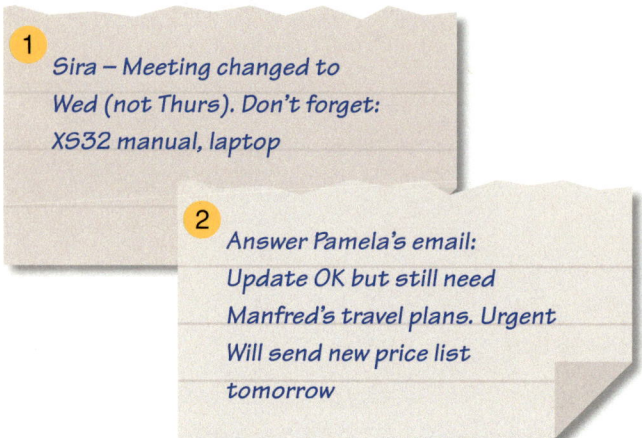

1 Sira – Meeting changed to
Wed (not Thurs). Don't forget:
XS32 manual, laptop

2 Answer Pamela's email:
Update OK but still need
Manfred's travel plans. Urgent
Will send new price list
tomorrow

3 Email Johann with update
(check with Alice to make sure
he's back from holiday) YES!
Still no answer from Izumi about
the Appleton account.
Gantor-Brooks acct has been
approved
Meeting with me, Paul and Izumi
next week (Thursday 9 am)
if he has time?

OUTBOX

Cecil Armstrong is a trainer for office communication. In this text from his website he talks about one of his 'pet hates' – something which annoys him when he is using email as a communication tool.

Pet hate #3 – Over-quoting

"Something which really irritates me is over-quoting. This happens when someone adds comments to a long email without deleting any of the previous message. This makes the recipient's job very difficult, as s/he has to read the whole message again to find the one or two short comments which were made.

So, to avoid irritating your colleagues, here is a good tip to remember. If there are several important points to reply to, select these sentences or paragraphs, insert your comments after them and delete everything else. You could even put your text in a different colour so it's clear which parts of the email are from the original message and which are your comments. (Most email programs do this automatically.)

If you leave the original message exactly as you received it and just add a quick comment to the top, it looks like you haven't really read the message. If I were writing a book on email etiquette, this would be rule number one: keep all e-correspondence to one page or less and only quote relevant information.

Over to you

What do you think about quoting in emails? Do you ever do it?
Does it bother you as much as it does Cecil?
Is there anything which really annoys you when you receive emails? Write a list of 'five things NOT to do'.

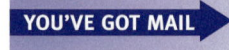

YOU'VE GOT MAIL   ▶   UNIT 5   Partner A   page 49
Partner B   page 51

Making and confirming arrangements

The domain name is the part of the email address which comes after the 'at' sign (@).
Find the part of the domain for someone who ...

.ac.uk @ .at @ .au @ .ca @ .ch @
.co.uk @ .com @ .net @ .es @ .gov @
.ibm.de @ .org

1 works for a company which is probably in the US.

2 works for a German division of a computer hardware company.

3 is writing from Australia.

4 is writing from Austria.

5 works for a non-profit organization.

6 works for a British university.

7 works for an Internet service provider.

8 lives in Switzerland.

9 is writing from Canada.

10 works for the US government.

11 is writing from Spain.

12 works for a company in England.

Now match the country codes to the countries (1–20).

.al @ .at @ .by @
.cz @ .dk @ .ee @
.fr @ .gr @ .ie @ .it
@ .lu @ .nl @ .no @
.pl @ .pt @ .se @ .si
@ .sk @ .tr @ .ua

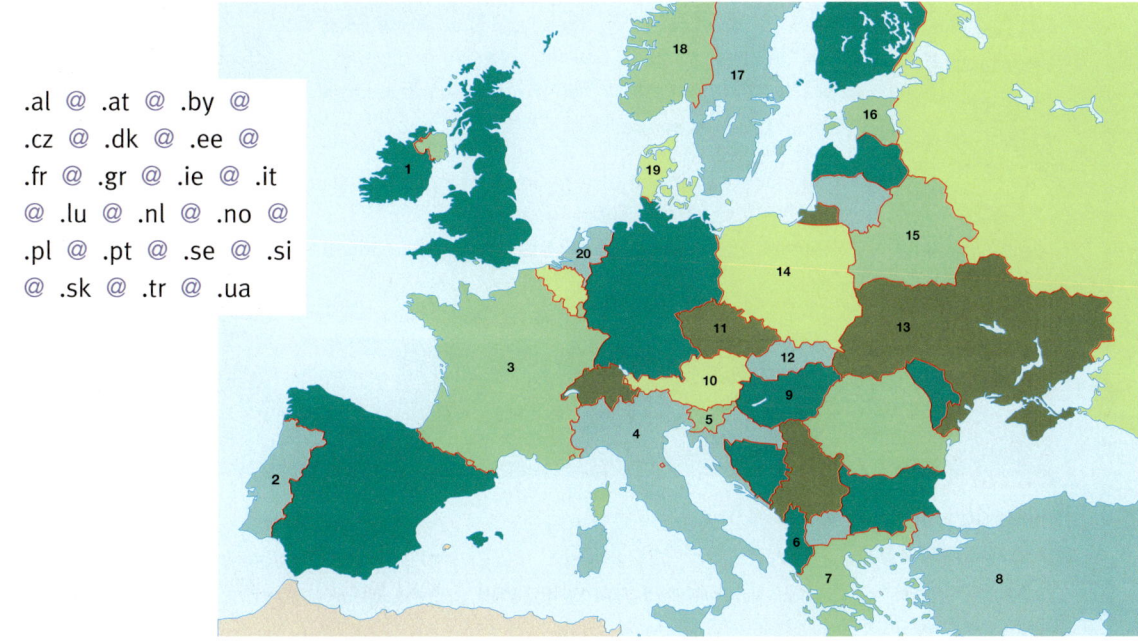

1   Below are two email exchanges. Match the emails with their replies.

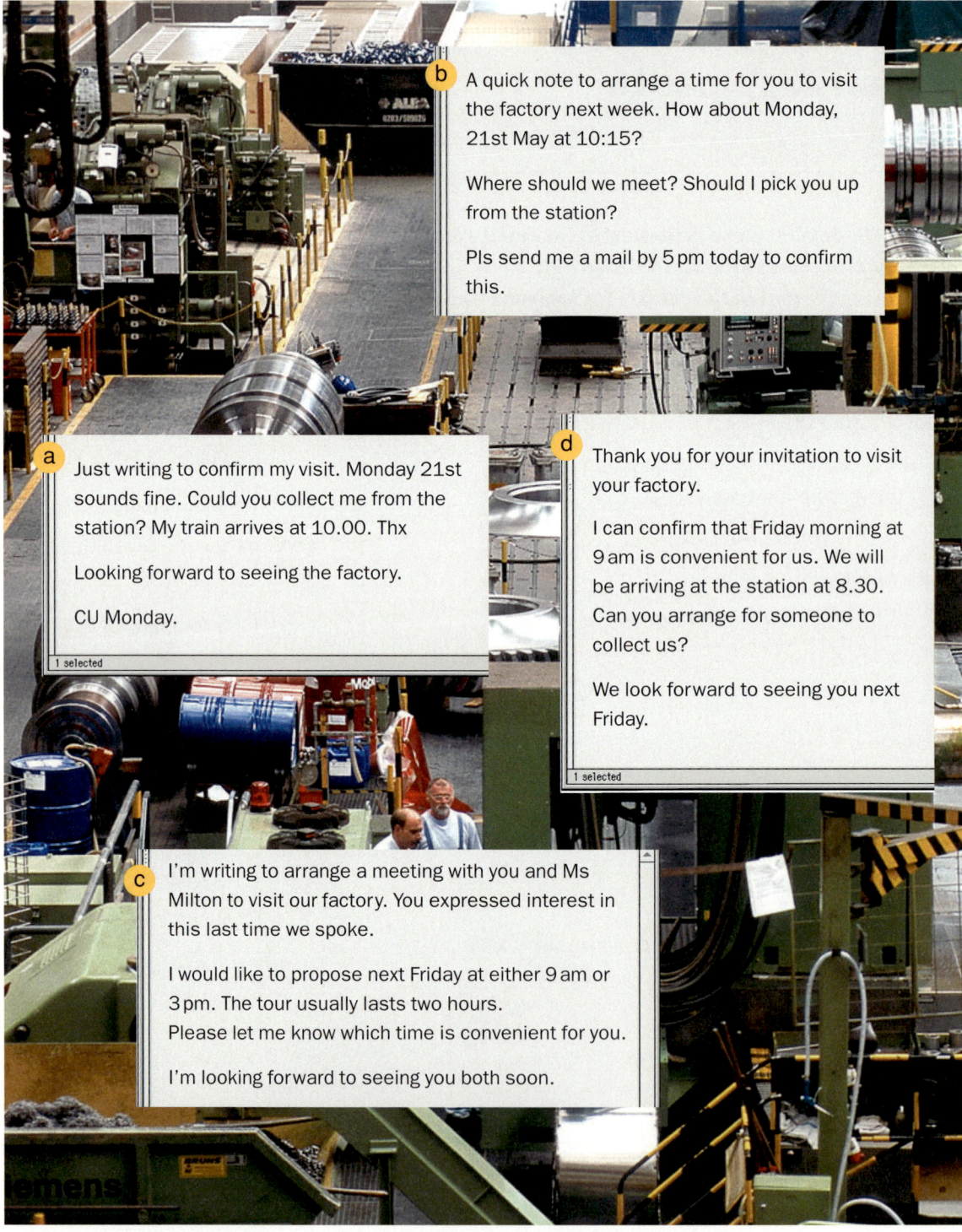

b A quick note to arrange a time for you to visit the factory next week. How about Monday, 21st May at 10:15?

Where should we meet? Should I pick you up from the station?

Pls send me a mail by 5 pm today to confirm this.

d Thank you for your invitation to visit your factory.

I can confirm that Friday morning at 9 am is convenient for us. We will be arriving at the station at 8.30. Can you arrange for someone to collect us?

We look forward to seeing you next Friday.

1 selected

a Just writing to confirm my visit. Monday 21st sounds fine. Could you collect me from the station? My train arrives at 10.00. Thx

Looking forward to seeing the factory.

CU Monday.

1 selected

c I'm writing to arrange a meeting with you and Ms Milton to visit our factory. You expressed interest in this last time we spoke.

I would like to propose next Friday at either 9 am or 3 pm. The tour usually lasts two hours.
Please let me know which time is convenient for you.

I'm looking forward to seeing you both soon.

VOCABULARY ASSISTANT

to collect sb [BE] *abholen*   to express interest *Interesse zeigen*
invitation *Einladung*   to pick sb up *abholen*   to propose *vorschlagen*

2 **Find phrases in the emails in exercise 1 to complete the gaps.**

Making arrangements

Organizing a date and a time

I'm writing to _ar_____ [1] .

A quick note to _ar_____ [2] to meet.

Just writing to organize a time for your visit.
When would suit you best?
What about 5 o'clock?

_H_____ [3] Tuesday?
Is 5 o'clock suitable?
Is Tuesday convenient?
Is 3 pm OK?

Please let me know _wh_____ [4] .

Please let me know if this is convenient.

Organizing a meeting place

Where should _w_____ [5] ?

Should I _p_____ [6] from the station?

Should I collect you from the airport?

Could you _c_____ [7] ?

Could you arrange for _s_____ [8] ?
Meet me at the station.
I'll see you at reception.

Confirming arrangements

I'd like to confirm my visit.

Just writing to _c_____ [9] the arrangements.

I can confirm that 9 am is _c_____ [10] .
I'd prefer Friday at 8 am.
5 o'clock is good for me/is fine.
Tuesday sounds great/suits me.
Let me know if this is OK.
Please send me an email by 5 pm today _to c_____ [11] .
I look forward to meeting you.

_L_____ [12] seeing the factory.
See you on Tuesday!

3   **Use the phrases below to complete the two emails.**

good for me @ I look forward to @ Is 12.30 OK @ send me an email @ to confirm @ what about @ writing to arrange

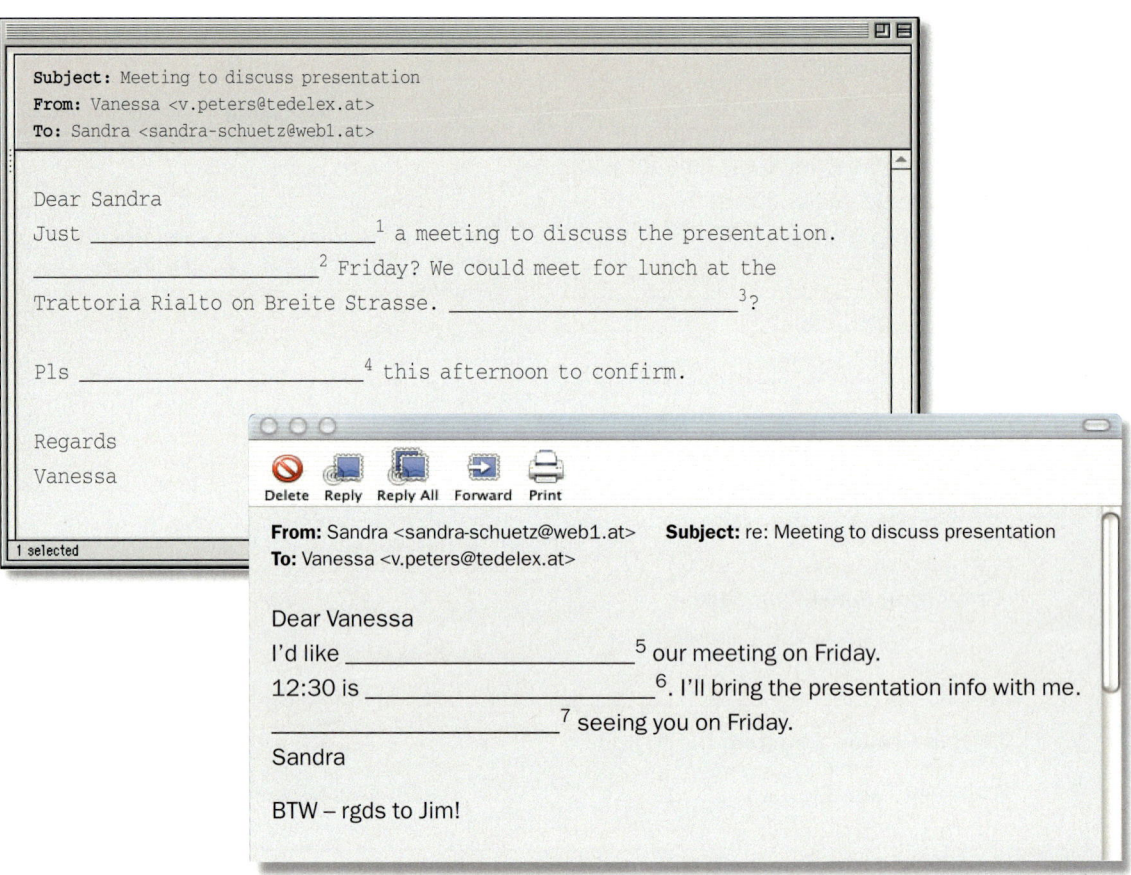

Subject: Meeting to discuss presentation
From: Vanessa <v.peters@tedelex.at>
To: Sandra <sandra-schuetz@web1.at>

Dear Sandra
Just _____[1] a meeting to discuss the presentation.
_____[2] Friday? We could meet for lunch at the
Trattoria Rialto on Breite Strasse. _____[3]?

Pls _____[4] this afternoon to confirm.

Regards
Vanessa

1 selected

From: Sandra <sandra-schuetz@web1.at>   **Subject:** re: Meeting to discuss presentation
To: Vanessa <v.peters@tedelex.at>

Dear Vanessa
I'd like _____[5] our meeting on Friday.
12:30 is _____[6]. I'll bring the presentation info with me.
_____[7] seeing you on Friday.
Sandra

BTW – rgds to Jim!

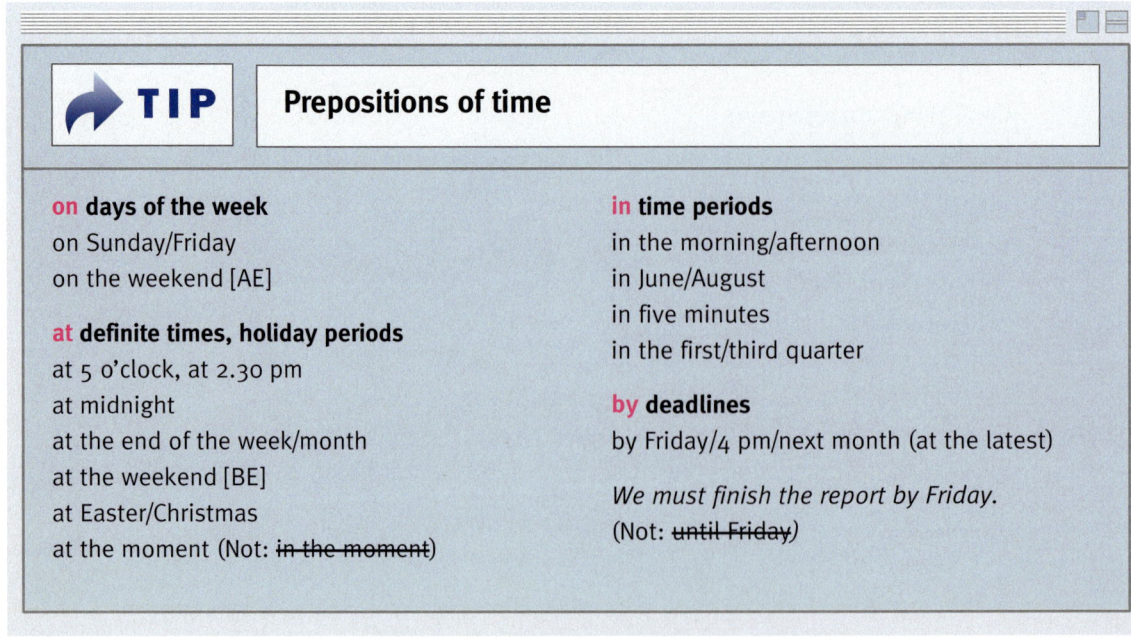

TIP   **Prepositions of time**

on days of the week
on Sunday/Friday
on the weekend [AE]

at definite times, holiday periods
at 5 o'clock, at 2.30 pm
at midnight
at the end of the week/month
at the weekend [BE]
at Easter/Christmas
at the moment (Not: ~~in the moment~~)

in time periods
in the morning/afternoon
in June/August
in five minutes
in the first/third quarter

by deadlines
by Friday/4 pm/next month (at the latest)

We must finish the report by Friday.
(Not: ~~until Friday~~)

4 Read the following sentences and cross out the incorrect prepositions.

1 The conference begins ~~at~~ / on / ~~in~~ Monday at / on / in the afternoon.

2 Could you pick me up at / with / on 5 o'clock?

3 The report must be finished in / by / at Tuesday.

4 All holidays must be taken at / on / in June.

5 The company was founded by / in / on 2001.

6 I'll be at a client's in / at / on the end of the week.

7 On / In / At the moment I'm very busy but I'll be able to finish the report by / until / on next week.

8 If I haven't heard from you by / in / at the weekend, I'll call you in / on / at Saturday.

5 Use the notes below to write an email to a client to set up a meeting.

> Tues
>
> second meeting to finalize terms and conditions next week
>
> three possible times:
>
> > Monday 13/3 2 pm
> >
> > Thursday 16/3, any time
> >
> > Friday 17/3 morning any time
>
> need approx 2 hours
>
> (Urgent: deadline for reserving conference room tomorrow noon!)

6 Now look at the client's diary and write a response.

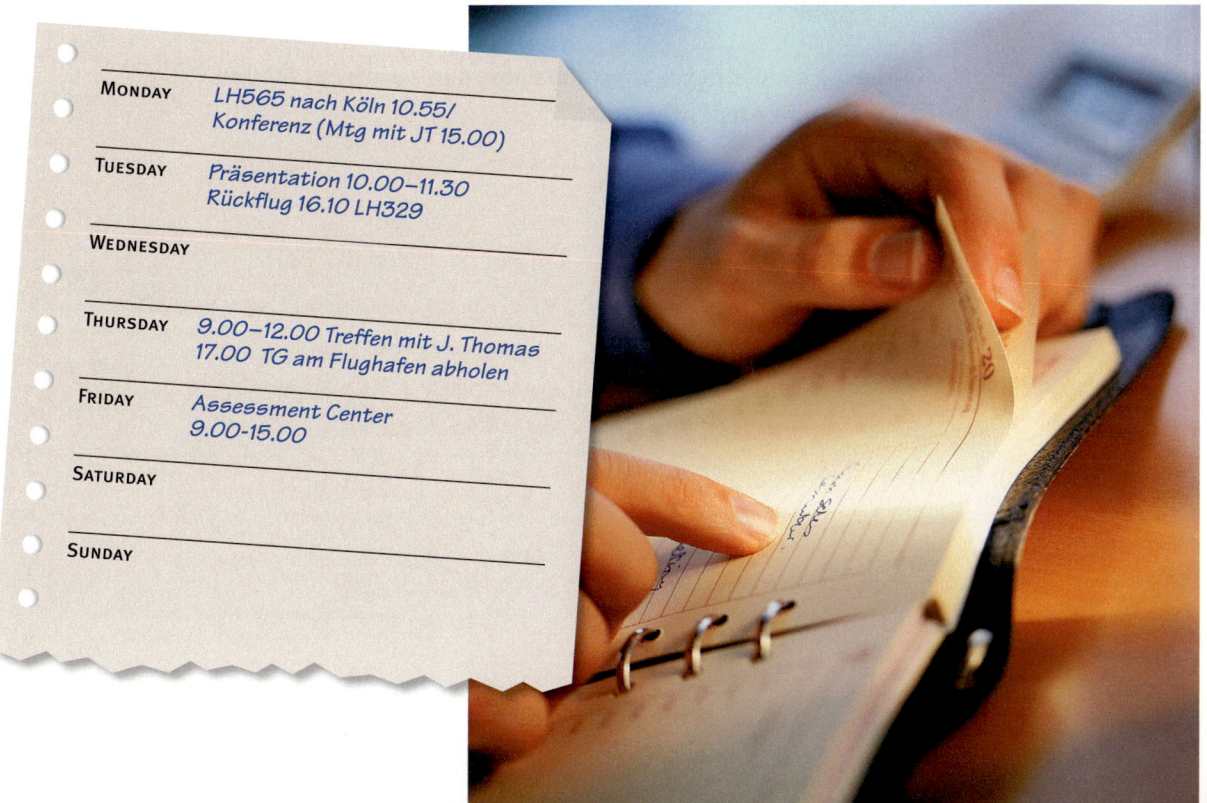

MONDAY LH565 nach Köln 10.55/
Konferenz (Mtg mit JT 15.00)

TUESDAY Präsentation 10.00–11.30
Rückflug 16.10 LH329

WEDNESDAY

THURSDAY 9.00–12.00 Treffen mit J. Thomas
17.00 TG am Flughafen abholen

FRIDAY Assessment Center
9.00–15.00

SATURDAY

SUNDAY

7　**Nigel Sharp receives the following reply to an email he sent. What words or expressions does Christiane use to:**

1　say that the suggested dates are not convenient? Find two examples.
2　say that she's sorry? Find two examples.
3　suggest changing the meeting to a later date?
4　suggest a new time to meet?

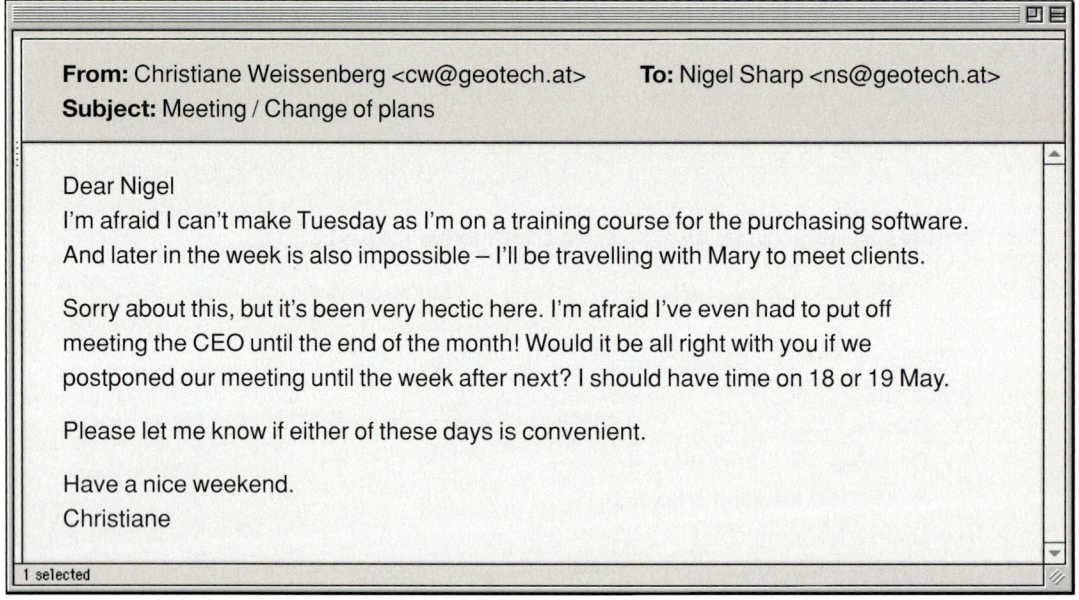

From: Christiane Weissenberg <cw@geotech.at>　　**To:** Nigel Sharp <ns@geotech.at>
Subject: Meeting / Change of plans

Dear Nigel
I'm afraid I can't make Tuesday as I'm on a training course for the purchasing software. And later in the week is also impossible – I'll be travelling with Mary to meet clients.

Sorry about this, but it's been very hectic here. I'm afraid I've even had to put off meeting the CEO until the end of the month! Would it be all right with you if we postponed our meeting until the week after next? I should have time on 18 or 19 May.

Please let me know if either of these days is convenient.

Have a nice weekend.
Christiane

1 selected

VOCABULARY ASSISTANT　　CEO *geschäftsführende/r Direktor/in*　client *Kunde/Kundin*　to make (an appointment) *hier: einen Termin einhalten*　to postpone *verschieben*

8　**You receive the following email but the time and dates don't work out for you. Use the words below to write a reply.**

I'm afraid @ postpone @ by Monday @ would it be all right @ can't make it

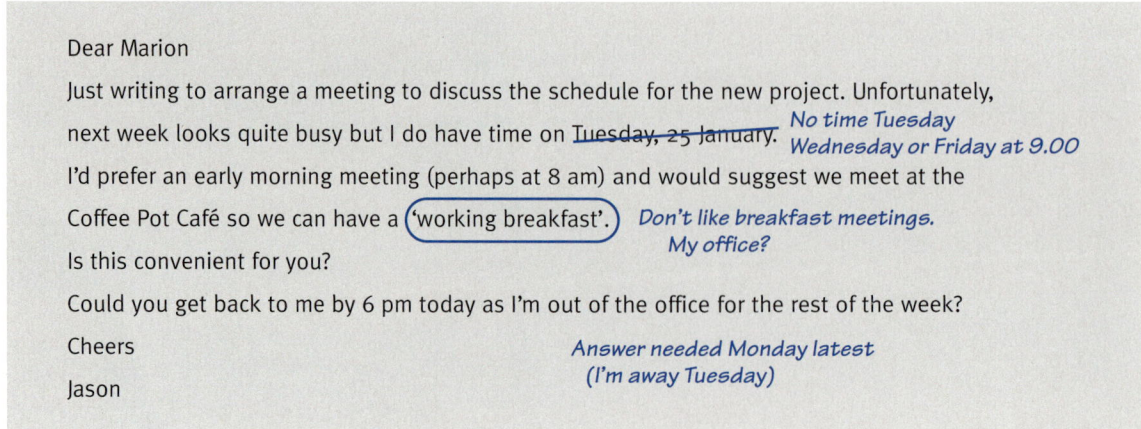

Dear Marion

Just writing to arrange a meeting to discuss the schedule for the new project. Unfortunately, next week looks quite busy but I do have time on ~~Tuesday, 25 January.~~ *No time Tuesday Wednesday or Friday at 9.00*

I'd prefer an early morning meeting (perhaps at 8 am) and would suggest we meet at the

Coffee Pot Café so we can have a 'working breakfast'. *Don't like breakfast meetings. My office?*
Is this convenient for you?

Could you get back to me by 6 pm today as I'm out of the office for the rest of the week?

Cheers

Jason　　*Answer needed Monday latest (I'm away Tuesday)*

Read this article and answer the questions.

Have you been spammed!?

'Spamming' is when a company sends you its advertising material via email without your consent. These emails are the electronic equivalent of junk mail. The first example of junk mail was by companies using the conventional postal service to send flyers and advertising leaflets about their products in the form of mail shots to postal addresses. Nowadays, if you have bought anything via the Internet, particularly from the US, it's common to be bombarded with spams from other companies. Your email address gets passed on to a mailing list and then suddenly you're getting several emails daily encouraging you to buy something or sign up on website shopping sites. Internet research company Jupiter

Media Metrix predicts consumers will receive about 206 billion junk emailings by 2006 – an average of 1,400 per person. Each piece of spam is said to cost $1 in lost productivity. To combat this unwanted form of advertising, California has even introduced an anti-spam law requiring companies to provide a free-phone number or a link/place on their website for you to take your name off their mailing list. At the moment an email marketing company in Silicon Valley is being challenged in court for its spamming activities and the law company representing spammed companies is demanding $50 per email sent! An expensive business if the claimants win.

Over to you

Do you receive spams? If so, what do you do with them?
How can companies stop junk mail from entering their systems?
Do you think there should be stricter regulations regarding junk mail?

YOU'VE GOT MAIL ➜ UNIT 5   Partner A   page 49
  Partner B   page 51

Test yourself!

See how much you've learned about writing emails in English.
Use the clues to complete the crossword puzzle.

Across

2 A word meaning 'the latest date to finish something, like a report'.
5 'to make clear': *I'm writing to … the terms of the agreement.*
7 An abbreviated expression for 'as fast as you can'.
10 electronic junk mail
12 To give sb the most recent information: *Just writing to … you on the changes.*
13 You do this when you send an email you've received to a third person.
15 'to make contact': *This is to … base before the conference.*
17 'bestätigen': *This is to … the date of our meeting.*
20 You do this when you want to remove a message from your inbox.
21 A way to start an email: *… a quick note to say hi.*
22 Another word for 'answer': *Looking forward to your … .*
23 Another word for 'happy': *We would be … if you could send us … .*
27 Complete the phrase: *Sorry I can't … Thursday. How about Monday?*
28 The eleventh character in this email address: info@trans-com.at
29 The fifteenth character in the above address.

Down

1 An informal email salutation.
3 Another way to say 'inform me' (3 words): *Please … if you need anything else.*
4 A preposition used to talk about deadlines: *I need the report … Monday.*
6 A polite way to say something unpleasant: *I'm … I haven't done the report yet.*
7 A document you send using email.
8 The missing word: *We are having a few problems … the moment.*
9 The sixth character in this email address: carol_banks@gt.ch
11 You do this to an appointment when you move it to a later date.
13 You can write this in your subject line or at the beginning of an email to show you just want to give information and don't expect a reply.
14 Another, more formal word for 'help'.
16 If you delay a project or a decision, you 'put it on …'.
18 Two letters used to introduce the subject of an email.
19 The full form of 'pls'.
24 A standard close to a more formal email.
25 'dringend': *I would appreciate a reply asap as the matter is quite … .*
26 A way to end an email when you want a reply: *Looking forward to … from you.*

Now fill in the letters from the puzzle to find a final tip for writing a good, accurate email.

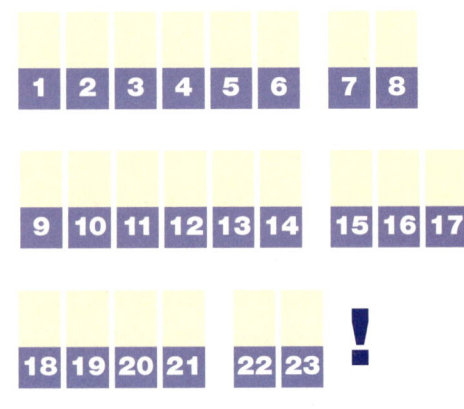

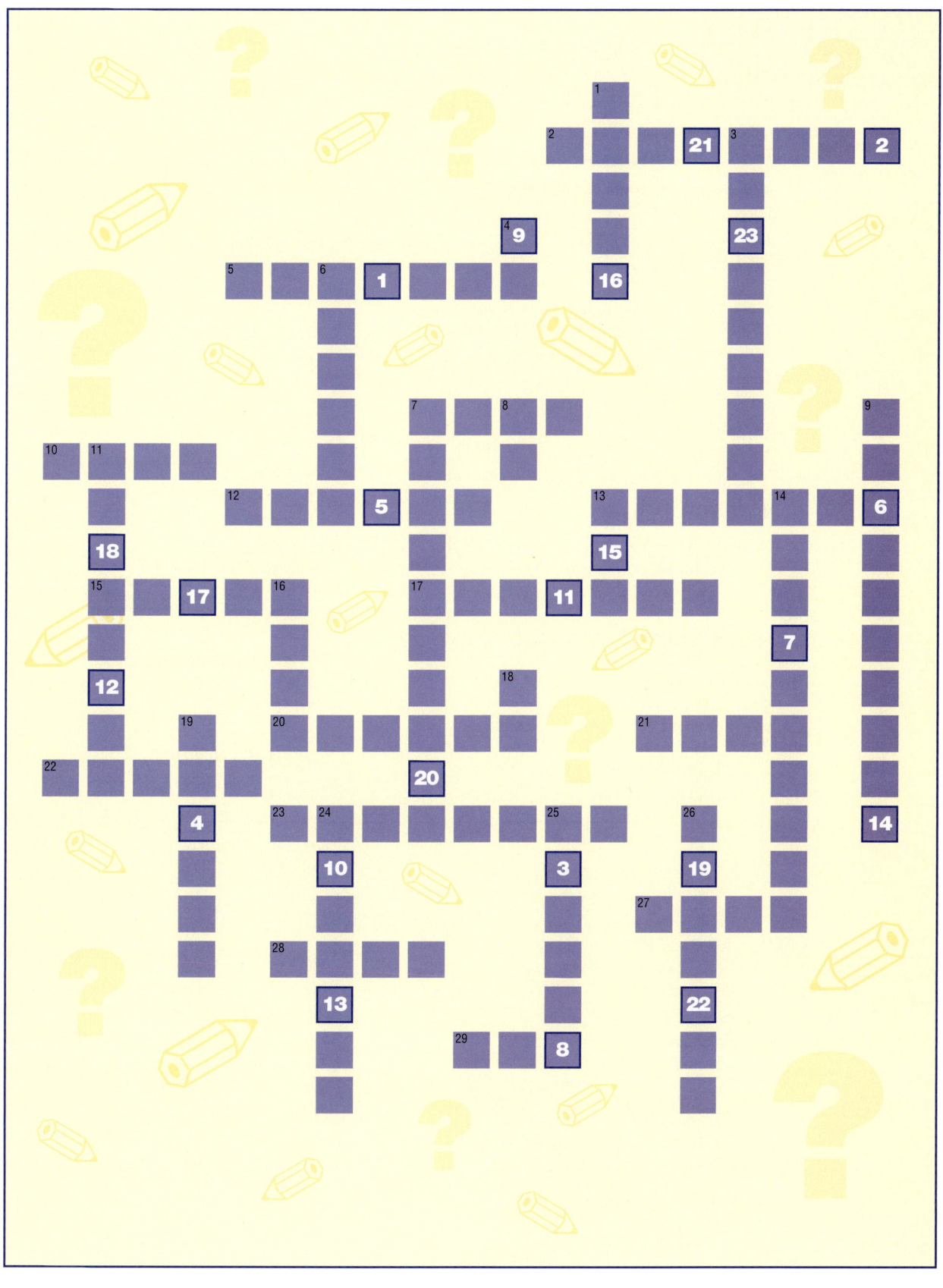

Partner A You've got mail!

General instructions
Follow the instruction under each unit heading to *write* an email. Then exchange emails with Partner B and *reply* to his or her email. Check the instructions again for extra information.

Unit 1 An introduction to emails

Write
Write a short email to a colleague. Tell him/her about Steven Rosenstein's retirement party.

Invitation

Friday 20th August

6 pm

at Joey's Bar

Reply
Thank your supplier for the information.

Unit 2 Formal & informal emails

Write
Your boss left this post-it note on your desk while you were at lunch. Follow the instructions she gave you.

> *Bitte Email an Ronald Chambers schicken: r.chambers@jsu.com*
>
> *Wir haben weder ihre Telefon-nummer noch eine Lieferadresse, aber brauchen sie für unsere Klientendatenbank.*
>
> *Übrigens sie sind neue Klienten und haben noch keinen Vertrag mit uns!*
>
> *Danke!*
> *Jan*

Reply
You receive an email from a former colleague. Reply to it.

Unit 3 Enquiries

Write
You receive the information below. Write an email to Brian, but remember, you've only met him once at a trade fair and exchanged business cards.

> *Can you ask that guy Brian who you met at the last international trade fair if he can send us some info about their new product? It would be great if he could give us a demo too!*
>
> *Thanks! Kirsten*

Reply
You work at a hotel and receive an email. Write a reply to it.

> ### Our Facilities
>
> 4 large meeting rooms, 1 seats 60 people, 1 seats 40 people, 2 seat 20 people
>
> Technical support
>
> Swimming pool and sauna
>
> Restaurant (weekends – restaurant only open evenings; for lunchtime arrangements our staff are happy to reserve you a table at a local restaurant)
>
> Internet access in residents' lounge

Unit 4   Requesting action

Write

Write an email to your colleague requesting action. You need:

- 2 quarterly reports (regions 1 & 2), deadlines end of week & middle of next week
- information about competitor's new product
- minutes of last meeting

Reply

You receive an email from a customer. Reply to it, using the information below.

Order form

1. 25 white radiators, style "Richmond", item no. RI 539
2. 5 glass shower cabinets, style "Estelle", item no. ES 651
3. 12 oval mirrors with light, style "Helio", item no. HE 824
4. 6 bathroom cabinets – pine, style "Rustic", item no. RU 418
5. 10 shower taps, style "Nostalgia", item no. NO 332
6. 7 towel rails – chrom, style "Moderne", item no. MO 739

1) already sent – arrival end of week 12th Feb approx

2+3) not in stock

4) to be sent tomorrow – 9th Feb, take 2 weeks to arrive

5) already sent – arrival end of week 12th Feb approx

6) will be sent next week – arrival approx. 3 weeks – 2nd March

Unit 5   Exchanging information

Write

Read the information on the note and put it into an email.

> Could you let Willi know about the promotion dates (5 – 15th January)? Ask him if he's got the market research results back & send him the packaging design.
>
> Cheers
> Sid

Reply

Reply to the email you have received.

Unit 6   Making and confirming arrangements

Write

You need to set up a meeting with your colleague to discuss a new promotion. The meeting will take about two hours. Write an email to your colleague to arrange this. Use the diary below to decide when you can meet.

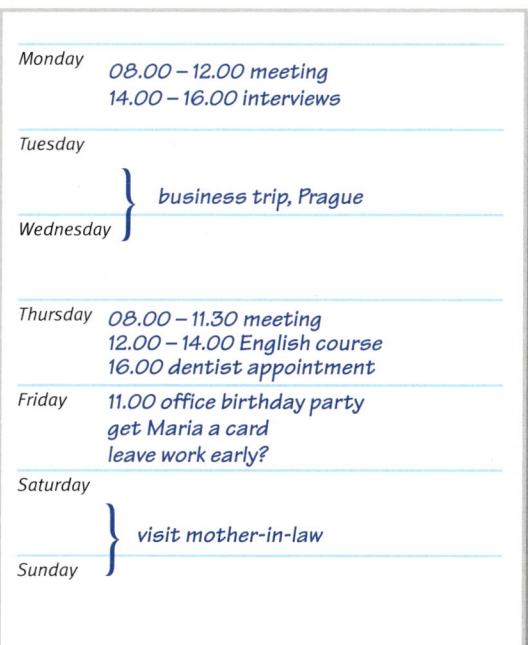

Monday	08.00 – 12.00 meeting 14.00 – 16.00 interviews
Tuesday	business trip, Prague
Wednesday	
Thursday	08.00 – 11.30 meeting 12.00 – 14.00 English course 16.00 dentist appointment
Friday	11.00 office birthday party get Maria a card leave work early?
Saturday	visit mother-in-law
Sunday	

Reply

Reply to the email, confirming the date. The time is too early, suggest a later time and a location.

Partner B   You've got mail!

General instructions

Follow the instruction under each unit heading to *write* an email. Then exchange emails with Partner B and *reply* to his or her email. Check the instructions again for extra information.

Unit 1   An introduction to emails

Write

Write an email to a client. You have some new brochures, which will be in the post today. The prices have changed though!

Reply

Thank your colleague for the reminder. You're definitely going. Keep the email short.

Unit 2   Formal & informal emails

Write

You receive this memo at work.

---

memo

Dear Colleagues
We're pleased to announce that Carol has been promoted to head the Logistics Department, beginning March 1. We're sure you'll join us in congratulating her & wishing her good luck!

You worked with Carol for many years before changing departments. Send her an email.

Reply

You receive an email from your potential supplier. Reply to it using the following information.

To: Purchasing Dept
From: Management (Jakob Leitner)

Message:
Due to warehouse location change, our delivery address is now:
Avenida Diagonal, 643
08034 Barcelona
Spain
Tel. no. +34 93 280 4923
Please make sure NOTHING is sent to this address until 1st July.
JL

Unit 3   Enquiries

Write

You are organizing a small conference and would like to receive an offer from a few hotels.
Use the information below to write an enquiry.

- Dates: Saturday & Sunday (3rd & 4th Sept)
- Participants: 45
- 10 participants need rooms
- buffet at lunchtime
- 3 meeting rooms for 15–20 people

Reply

Reply to the email you receive. You remember meeting the writer and can do what he/she asks.

Unit 4   Requesting action

Write

You have waited three weeks for an order of goods, which should have been with the forwarders last week. Send an email, asking your supplier to send you a list of what has already been sent & the expected arrival date.
Your original order is below.

Order form
- 25 white radiators, style "Richmond", item no. RI 539
- 5 glass shower cabinets, style "Estelle", item no. ES 651
- 12 oval mirrors with light, style "Helio", item no. HE 824
- 6 bathroom cabinets – pine, style "Rustic", item no. RU 418
- 10 shower taps, style "Nostalgia", item no. NO 332
- 7 towel rails – chrome, style "Moderne", item no. MO 739

Reply

You receive an email from one of your colleagues. Look at your 'to do' list and reply to it.

> write reports: region 1 ✔
> region 2 *still need figures from Tom*
> find out about competition ✔
> minutes of last meeting *finish next week*

Unit 5   Exchanging information

Write

Send an email to your team, informing them when you are on holiday. Tell them who will be the contact person while you're away and also ask them for their holiday dates so you can put them in the diary.

Reply

Reply to the email you have received using the information below.

> **Summary of Market Research Results:**
>
> Product "Minty" sweets
> 1. Design: can remain the same, was liked by testers
> 2. Strength of flavour: consumers complained, mint too hot!
> 3. Size: make slightly smaller, reduce amount to 25g
> 4. Advertising: fine! Positive feedback, especially the trial packs
>
> *Pls thank for packaging design attachment! Looks good!*

Unit 6   Making and confirming arrangements

Write

Write to a client, suggesting a date & time to meet (add your own details). You would like him/her to suggest the place.

Reply

You receive an email. Can you meet on the day suggested? Reply, either confirming or suggesting another date.
Use the diary below.

MONDAY	*trade fair*
TUESDAY	*trade fair*
WEDNESDAY	*09.00 doctor's appointment* *11.00 –13.00 lunch appointment with French visitors* *14.00 – 16.00 update meeting*
THURSDAY	
FRIDAY	*08.00 – 09.00 breakfast at Hotel Metropol*
SATURDAY	
SUNDAY	*camping with the kids*

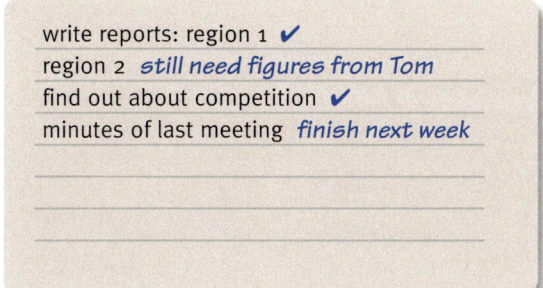 **Unit 2**

First write down the email and website addresses that your partner dictates.

1 _____

2 _____

3 _____

4 _____

5 _____

Then dictate these addresses to your partner:

6 http://news.bcj.co.uk
7 biz.bod@fnc.com
8 www.blc_clf.at
9 tt-dant@blackley.fr
10 HarlieJoy.xr@dante.it

Answer key

Unit 1

page 5

INBOX
(Suggested answers – open for discussion!)

1 Agree and disagree: On the one hand, emails and letters are both written forms of communication so you need some of the same basic language skills to write them well, eg good organization, clear and concise language, correct grammar and appropriate vocabulary. On the other hand, emails *are* different to letters in terms of style, register and language used so you need some different skills as well. This book will help you develop the language skills needed to write good emails in English.

2 Agree and disagree: It is true that emails (especially informal ones) share some of the same vocabulary and style as spoken messages. But this type of informal language is not usually suitable when writing emails in a professional context. (See Unit 2 *Formal & informal emails*.)

3 Agree: Not only is the subject line useful for telling the recipient what the email is about before it is read, but it is also helpful for finding the email later when it is filed away in the inbox. (See exercise 4 on page 8.)

4 Agree: You might find native speakers do not always correct mistakes in their emails. This can be acceptable – especially in internal emails – as long as the mistakes do not interfere with communication. On the other hand, even if the message is clear, too many mistakes can give a bad impression. (See OUTBOX on page 17 for discussion.)

5 Agree and disagree: Copying others in to your email exchange does help keep everybody informed about what is happening or what decisions have been made (and might even reduce the time spent in meetings!). But the option is often overused and can waste people's time when they have to read a lot of emails every day. (See OUTBOX on page 31 for discussion.)

6 Agree: As an email is received within minutes or even seconds, the writer usually expects an immediate response, even if it is just to say that the email has arrived and will be answered later.

7 Agree and disagree: It *is* more direct to reach for the phone, but with email you have the information in writing. Furthermore, you may pick an inconvenient time when you phone somebody, whereas an email can be read and answered when the other person has time.

page 6

1
1	inbox	8	forward
2	outbox	9	send/receive
3	sent items	10	contacts
4	drafts	11	high priority
5	deleted items	12	attachment
6	reply	13	subject
7	reply to all		

2
1 In 'sent items'.
2 In the inbox.
3 With the 'forward' command.
4 In 'contacts'.
5 In 'drafts'.
6 In the subject line.
7 With the 'high priority' command.
8 In the attachment.

3 Differences are: the salutation (*Hello* instead of *Dear*); the use of informal language and abbreviations (*hope* instead of *I hope* or *info* for *information*); close (*Regards* instead of *With best regards* or *Yours sincerely*); use of subject line; layout; the length (shorter and more concise than a letter), use of contracted forms (*haven't* for *have not*, *here's* for *here is*).

page 8

4
1	e	4	e	7	h		
2	c	5	f	8	l		
3	a	6	i	9	j or k		

5 **Model answers**
1 REQ: new production schedule
2 re: handbook XL20 motor
3 holiday from 3–5 Oct
4 meeting: time change
5 REQ: staff guidelines
6 Confirmation of order no 66193F/2

page 9

6

	Formal email	Informal email
salutation	h	e
opening sentence	g	b
body	a	i
friendly ending	j	c
close	d	f

page 10

7
1 regards
2 outbox
3 subject
4 forward
5 receive
6 high priority
7 message
8 reply
9 inbox
10 writing

The hidden word is **attachment**.

Unit 2

page 11

INBOX
1 c
2 d
3 f
4 g
5 b
6 a
7 e
8 :-)
9 O:-)
10 :-O
11 :-(
12 :->
13 ;-)
14 :-I

pages 12–13

1 The formal emails are a, c, d, f.
The informal emails are b, e.

page 13

2
1 f
2 b
3 e
4 c
5 d
6 a

page 14

3 Suggested answer

More formal	Less formal (or informal)
salutations & closes	
Dear Mr Braithwaite	Hey Gary!
Yours sincerely	Hello Gabi
Regards	See ya
Kind regards	Have a nice day
Thank you for your cooperation.	
phrases & vocabulary	
We would also appreciate …	I'm off to …
Please could you …	Just a note to tell you …
	Would it be OK if …
(following can also be used in informal emails)	Hope you …
	Speak to you …
I'm writing to …	
Thank you for …	tell (instead of 'inform')
I would like to …	put off (a visit) (instead of 'postpone')
	trouble (instead of 'inconvenience')
to inform	
to confirm	
to enquire	
to appreciate	

More formal	Less formal (or informal)
abbreviations, etc	
rep	info
	rep, memo (can also be used in formal emails)
	&
	:-)

page 15

4
2 help
3 to tell
4 to answer
5 to be sorry
6 to get in touch with
7 to put off
8 to set up
9 to ask
10 to need

5
1 enquire
2 require
3 arrange
4 inform
5 convenient
6 contact
7 sorry
8 put off
9 need
10 ask
11 set up
12 get in touch

page 16

6
2 as soon as possible
3 Thursday
4 January
5 at the moment
6 Best wishes
7 attention
8 regards
9 please
10 weekend

7 Email 1 is informal. It contains a colloquial phrase (*a bit of info*), abbreviations *(pls)*, an emoticon, an informal salutation *(Hi)* and no close. Furthermore some words are omitted (*I was wondering, I'm not sure*). See page 25 for more on this topic.

Email 2 is more formal. It contains a formal open and close (*Dear, Best regards*), more formal vocabulary (*attend, assist, arrange*) and no abbreviations or emoticons. Furthermore, although contractions are used (common in all emails), no words are omitted.

Model answers
Hi Teresa
Nice to hear from you.
The Hotel Bern is very central, but a bit expensive. It's OK if your company's paying! Otherwise, you could have a look at the following website address which has a lot of good hotels & B&Bs. The address is: www.berncityscope/accommodation/htm.
I'm sending you a map of Bern as an attachment so you can see where the hotels are.
Call me when you arrive so we can arrange to meet.
How about meeting for dinner instead of just a drink?
Looking forward to seeing you.
Bye for now
Johannes

Dear Sandy
Thanks for your email. You will find a good list of guest houses at the following address: www.berncityscope.ch/accommodation.htm. I think you can book online, which will save a lot of time. My parents stayed at Pension Bergland when they came to visit and I can recommend it. Alternatively, would you like me to book something for you? Let me know what you decide.
All the best
Johannes

page 17

8
1 Just
2 quick
3 tell
4 for the
5 I'll
6 touch
7 tomorrow's
8 off
9 See you
10 Regards

Dear Mahendra
We are still waiting for the above order but have received no email to explain the reason for the delay. This is particularly inconvenient for us at the moment as ~~as~~ our clients need the delivery asap. Please can you contact the forwarders to find out what has happened and inform us immediately? We look forward to hearing from you very soon.
Kind regards

Unit 3

page 18

INBOX

H	capital 'h'	.	dot
h	small 'h'	@	at
-	hyphen/dash	/	slash
_	underscore	\	back slash

page 19

1 Suggested answers
Advantages:
- Speed: Emails are faster to write and send than letters or faxes.
- Cost: Emails are cheaper than sending letters or phoning.
- Time to prepare: The message is in writing so you can prepare what you want to say (particularly important when responding to #2).
- Convenience: A phone call can be inconvenient for the person being called, especially if he or she works at a busy place like a travel agency (#3). An email (or a letter or fax) can be answered at the recipient's convenience.

Disadvantages:
- Accuracy: In contrast to a phone call, you need to take care when writing an email (or a letter). Mistakes which may be overlooked on the phone could give a bad impression when in writing. The impression you make is particularly important when responding to #2 (job advert).
- You might get more detailed information with a phone call – especially with adverts #1 and #3 – as you can react to what the person says and ask follow-up questions.

2 Correct order:

4b   1d   3a   2c

Model emails
Dear Ms Karlsson
I saw your advertisement for the position of receptionist at the Hotel Falkenberg in the Frankfurter Allgemeine Zeitung and am interested in applying for the job.
Could you please let me know if I can send my CV as an attachment or if you would prefer it by post? Also, do I need to fill in an application form?
I look forward to hearing from you.
Regards

Dear Sir or Madam
I saw your advert in the Yellow Pages, and am interested in a holiday in Ireland next spring.
Could you please send me a brochure with tourist information and a list of accommodation?
My address is …
I look forward to hearing from you soon.
Regards

page 20–21

3
1 Can you please send me … ?
2 Can you help?
3 Please answer asap.
4 Thanks for your email/request.
5 I'm sending you …
6 I'm sending you the … in an attachment.
7 We are working on your request.
8 We hope you are happy with this.
9 Thanks for choosing …
10 Let us know if you need any more help.

4
1 Could you please send
2 would you be able to help?
3 'd (or would) appreciate a reply asap.
4 Thank you for your email.
5 your request is being processed.
6 in an attachment.
7 hope you find this satisfactory.
8 Thank you for your interest. / Do not hesitate to contact us if you require further assistance.

page 22

5 Model answers
Our general manager saw your advert in yesterday's Financial Times and would be grateful if you could send her the free start-up packet advertised.

Could you please send it to the following address?

...

We would also appreciate any information you can send us on your after-sales service.

Thank you in advance.

T. Gerald

Dear Giovanni

Jane at headquarters gave me your name and said you could help me. I need some information about the upcoming trade fair in Milan.

1) Who is attending from the Milan office?

2) How many hotel rooms have you booked?

3) What time and where is the Tuesday night reception?

Please send me the information asap.

Regards

Martin

PS Could you please give me your extension number? I can't find it on the international list.

6 2 request   5 send   8 know
    3 asap   6 appreciate   9 interested
    4 satisfactory   7 enquiry   10 receive

7 Model answer

To: James Baker
From: (your name)
Subject: after-sales service brochures/English

Dear James

I'm the sales rep for Bigtop electric drills and saws in Saxony. Ute Müller gave me your name.

I am going to a trade fair in the Czech Republic next week and would like to order the English version of the after-sales service brochure. Could you please send me 1000 copies by Monday?

I would appreciate a reply asap.

Thank you for your help.

Regards

(your name)

page 23

8 Model answers

Dear Pia Stevens

Thank you for your enquiry about our range of office furniture 'progress'. The information you requested was sent by post this morning. It is also attached as a PDF file.

Please contact us if you need further assistance.

Regards

Dear Sandy Adams

Thank you for your email. The catalogue is in the post, and I have attached a list giving the addresses of all our stores so that you can see which is closest to you.

Please contact us if you need any more help.

Best wishes

Unit 4

page 25

INBOX

1 thanks
2 thank you (or thanks) in advance
3 regarding
4 frequently asked questions
5 see you!
6 for your information
7 regards
8 by the way
9 forward
10 request
11 in my opinion
12 all the best

1 I'm looking forward to seeing you next week.
2 Thank you in advance for your help.
3 I will be in touch tomorrow with the updated figures.
4 Please call me regarding our meeting on Thursday morning.
5 This is just a quick email to give you the new dates.
6 Have you got any exciting plans for the weekend?
7 There is no information on pay rises at the moment. I hope to hear something soon, though.

page 26

1 1 He'd like them all to send him the figures from the last quarter by first thing the next morning. He'd also like Pascal to coordinate a team and send through their report (by Thursday 4th). Barbara should finish and send the sales report (by Tuesday 2nd June) and Thilo should contact Hungary about the new account details (as soon as possible).

   2 Pascal has sent Simon the figures from the last quarter. She has also contacted her team and finished the sales figures. She hasn't finished the report as she and her team have been very busy.

   3 They seem to have a good working relationship and their emails are informal and friendly, although Simon writes slightly more formally, possibly because he's the boss.

page 27

2 Barbara's reply
   d Sorry, Simon, but I haven't finished the report yet.
   a Things have been so busy here that there hasn't been time to work on it.
   c Tuesday should be no problem though.
   b Last quarter's figures will be on your desk tomorrow a.m.

Thilo's reply
   g Simon, Anna at the Hungarian office has just sent the account details.
   f I've put a copy in the post already, but am sending it as an attachment too.
   e I've also attached the figures that you wanted.

page 28

3 1 will be
2 Have you ordered … yet
3 Have you contacted … yet
4 have you sent … yet
5 've just ordered
6 'll be delivered
7 've just had a look
8 Have you seen
9 'll forward
10 've left
11 hasn't called back yet
12 'll try
13 (will) ask
14 'll email

4 arrange an appointment, a meeting
attach a document, the minutes, a report
clarify details
demand payment
finalize details, the minutes, a report
inform colleagues
meet colleagues, a deadline
notify colleagues
schedule an appointment, a meeting, payment
send details, the minutes, payment, a report
update a database
write the minutes, a report

page 29

1 sending
2 inform
3 arranged (or scheduled)
4 clarify
5 deadline
6 finalize
7 update
8 payment

5 The questions and requests might have been:
2 I'd be interested to know what you think.
3 Can you also send me the statistics on Internet use in the company, please?
4 I haven't heard from Sanji for ages. Have you?
5 Do you have the dates of the next internal policies meeting?

Model answer
Dear Martin,
Could you send me a copy of the new Internet guidelines, please? I'd be interested to know what you think. Can you also send me the statistics on Internet use in the company, please?
BTW, I haven't heard from Sanji for ages. Have you? Any idea where she is?
One last thing – do you have the dates of the next internal policies meeting?
Many thanks!
Annika

page 30

6 Model answer
Dear Roger
I'm glad to hear the presentation went well.

First of all, Steve has agreed to do your presentation for you. I haven't corrected the overheads yet but will do so asap and give them to Steve.
Here's an update on what I've been doing while you've been away.
1) We've got an extension of 30 days from our suppliers.
2) I've booked a room at the International (the Hilton was not available) for the reception and have also received an offer for the buffet lunch. It's 50 euros a person. Is that OK?
3) I haven't renewed your parking permit yet but will do so by the end of the week.
4) Language courses have been arranged and I've informed the participants.
5) I haven't been able to reach Jeff yet (to cancel Friday) but I've left a message on his mailbox. I'll try again later.
6) Finally, I've spoken to Tessa about travel expenses, so that's OK.
Hope you have a successful meeting tomorrow.
All the best

Unit 5

page 33

1 1 Mike introduces the email with the subject line, 'Motorson invoice – the story continues!'. He then tells David he is giving him the low-down on the invoice to Motorson.
2 salutation: 'Hi David'
informing: from 'Here's the low-down …' to 'what do you think?'
stating the action to be taken: 'Could you call … ?'
giving a deadline: 'I'll need the info by Friday 12th …'
close: Cheers
3 The humour in the subject line – 'the story continues' – tells us that David already knows about the invoice. We also know that he already has a copy of the contract.
4 Mike has discovered that their contact person in the Finance Department has changed.
5 Mike asks David to call the company and find out the new details for the invoice, including who the new contact person is.

page 34

2 1 to look at sth in detail
2 to get in contact with sb
3 to send sth by post
4 to send sb an email
5 to give sb information
6 to try to find or get sth (that is missing)
7 to be out of touch or not have heard sth
8 to postpone sth (or put sth off)

Model answer
Hello Uta
Thanks for getting in touch and giving me the information/details on the March sales meeting. By the way, I called Birgit's office and tried to get the January figures but she's been on holiday – so no success there! Perhaps you could get in contact with Gerd and ask him to send me an email with the info directly. I hope he can – I'd hate to have to postpone the meeting.
Oh, one last thing: can you send me a few of the new brochures. No hurry – the post will do!
Ciao
Jon

page 35

3 1 We'll report
2 We're happy
3 Let's introduce, They've been
4 plant's
5 haven't received, I'll send
6 Here's, we'll have to, it's not

4 1 b 2 d 3 c 4 e 5 a

page 36

5 Informing
Here are the details on …
I'm writing to clarify …
I'd like to inform you of …
Just a few comments about/on …
Just to update you on …
Let me fill you in on …
You'll find the info attached …

Replying
I'll get back to you asap …
Thank you for clarifying …
I'll follow up the points mentioned in your email …
Thanks for your email.

6 1 to update you on
2 get back to you asap
3 like to inform you of
4 the info attached
5 reply to your email
6 for your email
7 me fill you in on

page 37

7 Model answer
Helen
We have a slight problem. I asked you to send me the conference details *last week* but I still haven't received them. Unfortunately, the hotel needs the info today or we will lose the reservation. The situation is rather serious as this is the only hotel available in Madstown for our dates and I don't want to have to change the conference location. Could you please take care of this immediately?
Thanks in advance.
Jack

page 38

8 Model answers
1 Hi Sira,
Just to let you know, the meeting is now on Wednesday (not Thursday as planned). Don't forget to bring the XS32 manual and a laptop!

2 Dear Pamela
Thanks for the update you sent. Yes, it's fine, but I still urgently need Manfred's travel plans. Please could you get them to me asap.
Also, I'll get back to you tomorrow with the new price list.
Thanks.

3 Hi Johann
Hope you had a good holiday!
To keep you updated: still nothing from Izumi about the Appleton account, but the Gantor-Brooks account has finally been approved.
If you can fit it in, I suggest a meeting with the two of us and Paul and Izumi next week. How about Thursday at 9.00? Let me know.

Unit 6

page 39

INBOX
1 .com
2 .ibm.de
3 .au
4 .at
5 .org
6 .ac.uk
7 .net
8 .ch
9 .ca
10 .gov
11 .es
12 .co.uk

1	.ie	Ireland	11	.cz	Czech Republic
2	.pt	Portugal	12	.sk	Slovakia
3	.fr	France	13	.ua	Ukraine
4	.it	Italy	14	.pl	Poland
5	.si	Slovenia	15	.by	Belarus
6	.al	Albania	16	.ee	Estonia
7	.gr	Greece	17	.se	Sweden
8	.tr	Turkey	18	.no	Norway
9	.hu	Hungary	19	.dk	Denmark
10	.at	Austria	20	.nl	Netherlands

page 40

1 **b** is the initial email, and **a** is the reply.
c is the initial email, and **d** is the reply.

page 41

2 1 arrange a meeting
2 arrange a time
3 How about
4 which time is convenient (for you)
5 we meet
6 pick you up
7 collect me/us
8 someone to collect me/us
9 confirm
10 convenient
11 to confirm this
12 Looking forward to

page 42

3 1 writing to arrange   5 to confirm
   2 What about   6 good for me
   3 Is 12:30 OK   7 I look forward to
   4 send me an email

page 43

4 1 in   3 by   5 in   7 At, by
   2 at   4 in   6 at   8 by, on

5 Model answer
Dear XXX
I am writing to arrange our second meeting to
finalize the terms and conditions of the contract. I
can suggest three possible times next week:
Monday, 13 March at 2 pm, Thursday, 16 March at
any time, or any time on Friday morning. I think
we'll need about two hours to cover everything.
Please let me know by tomorrow morning which
date is most convenient for you. I need to reserve
the conference room by noon.
Many thanks
Regards
YYY

6 Model answer
Dear YYY
Thanks for your email suggesting times for next
week's meeting. I'd prefer to meet on Thursday at
2 pm if that's OK with you.
Please send me a quick email to confirm this.
Looking forward to seeing you again.
Regards
XXX

page 44

7 1 I can't make …
     … later in the week is also impossible …
   2 I'm afraid …
     Sorry about this, …
   3 Would it be all right with you if we postponed
     our meeting …
   4 I should have time on …

8 Model answer
Hi Jason
Thanks for your email. I'm sorry to hear that we
have to postpone the meeting. I'm afraid I can't
make it on Tuesday, though. Could we meet at 9 am
on either Wednesday or Friday instead?
Also, would it be all right if we met in my office and
not at the café?
Please confirm the new date by Monday as I'll be
out of the office all day Tuesday.
Best wishes
Marion

pages 46–47

Test yourself!

Across		**Down**	
2	deadline	1	hello
5	clarify	3	let me know
7	asap	4	by
10	spam	6	afraid
12	update	7	attachment
13	forward	8	at
15	touch	9	underscore
17	confirm	11	postpone
20	delete	13	FYI
21	just	14	assistance
22	reply	16	hold
23	grateful	18	re
27	make	19	please
28	dash	24	regards
29	dot	25	urgent
		26	hearing

A final tip for writing good, accurate emails:
Reread it before you send it!

A–Z wordlist

A

abbreviation [ə,briːviˈeɪʃn]	Abkürzung
absence [ˈæbsəns]	Abwesenheit, Fehlen
access [ˈækses]	Zugang
accommodation [ə,kɒməˈdeɪʃn]	Unterkunft
according to [əˈkɔːdɪŋ tə]	zufolge, nach
account [əˈkaʊnt]	Konto, Kunde
accuracy [ˈækjərəsi]	Genauigkeit
acquaintance [əˈkweɪntəns]	Bekanntschaft
acronym [ˈækrənɪm]	Kurzwort
to **address sb** [əˈdres]	jdn anreden, ansprechen
advice [ədˈvaɪs]	(guter) Rat
amusing [əˈmjuːzɪŋ]	lustig, amüsant
angel [ˈeɪndʒəl]	Engel
angry [ˈæŋgri]	wütend, ärgerlich
to **announce** [əˈnaʊns]	ankündigen
announcement [əˈnaʊnsmənt]	Ankündigung, Durchsage
to **annoy** [əˈnɔɪ]	ärgern
apology [əˈpɒlədʒi]	Entschuldigung
apostrophe [əˈpɒstrəfi]	Apostroph
appointment [əˈpɔɪntmənt]	Termin, Verabredung
to **appreciate** [əˈpriːʃieɪt]	dankbar sein für
approx(imately) [əˈprɒksɪmətli]	ungefähr
arrangements [əˈreɪndʒmənts]	Pläne, Abmachungen
asap [,eɪ es eɪ ˈpiː]	so schnell wie möglich
assistance [əˈsɪstəns]	Hilfe, Unterstützung
attached [əˈtætʃt]	beigefügt
attachment [əˈtætʃmənt]	Anlage
to **attend** [əˈtend]	teilnehmen
automatically [,ɔːtəˈmætɪkli]	automatisch
available [əˈveɪləbl]	verfügbar
average [ˈævərɪdʒ]	Durchschnitt

B

ballpoint pen [,bɔːlpɔɪnt ˈpen]	Kugelschreiber
blind copy [,blaɪnd ˈkɒpi]	Blindband
to **bombard** [bɒmˈbaːd]	bombardieren
brochure [ˈbrəʊʃə]	Broschüre, Prospekt
bulletin [ˈbʊlətɪn]	Zeitschrift
business card [ˈbɪznəs kaːd]	(Visiten-)Karte
business trip [ˈbɪznəs trɪp]	Geschäftsreise

C

to **cancel** [ˈkænsl]	streichen, absagen
to **care** [keə]	sorgen, sich kümmern
careless [ˈkeələs]	nachlässig, sorglos
to **cause** [kɔːz]	machen, verursachen
to **challenge** [ˈtʃælɪndʒ]	auffordern, anfechten
character [ˈkærəktə]	Buchstabe
to **chase sth up** [,tʃeɪs ʌp, 'daʊn]	einer Sache nachgehen
chatroom [ˈtʃætruːm]	Forum
cheers (BE) [tʃɪəz]	danke
circumstances [ˈsɜːkəmstənsɪz]	Umstände
claimant [ˈkleɪmənt]	Anwärter/in, Anspruchsberechtigte/r
to **clarify** [ˈklærəfaɪ]	klären, klarstellen
clear [klɪə]	klar, deutlich
client [ˈklaɪənt]	Kunde, Kundin, Klient/in
close [kləʊz]	Schlussformel
colleague [ˈkɒliːg]	Kollege, Kollegin
to **collect sb** (BE) [kəˈlekt]	jdn abholen
colloquial [kəˈləʊkwiəl]	umgangssprachlich
to **combat** [ˈkɒmbæt]	kämpfen
comment, no ~ [nəʊ ˈkɒment]	kein Kommentar
competition [,kɒmpəˈtɪʃn]	Konkurrenz
to **complain** [kəmˈpleɪn]	(sich) beschweren, reklamieren
concerned [kənˈsɜːnd]	betroffen, besorgt
conclusion [kənˈkluːʒn]	(Schluss-)Folgerung
conference [ˈkɒnfərəns]	Konferenz, Besprechung
to **confirm** [kənˈfɜːm]	bestätigen

to **consent** [kənˈsent]	zustimmen
consultant [kənˈsʌltənt]	Berater/in
consumer [kənˈsjuːmə]	Verbraucher/in
to **contact** [ˈkɒntækt]	sich wenden an
contacts [ˈkɒntækts]	Kontakte, Verbindungen
contents [ˈkɒntents]	Inhalt
contract [ˈkɒntrækt]	Vertrag
contracted [kənˈtræktɪd]	gekürzt
convenient, to be ~ [bi kənˈviːniənt]	passend sein
conventional [kənˈvenʃənl]	herkömmlich, konventionell
cooperation [kəʊ,ɒpəˈreɪʃn]	Zusammenarbeit, Unterstützung
core-time [ˈkɔːtaɪm]	Kernzeit
corporate [ˈkɔːpərət]	Firmen-, Konzern-
correspondence [,kɒrɪˈspɒndəns]	Korrespondenz
court [kɔːt]	Gericht
cover letter [ˈkʌvə letə]	Begleitschreiben
to **crash** [kræʃ]	abstürzen
credit [ˈkredɪt]	Kredit, Gutschrift
current [ˈkʌrənt]	aktuell, gegenwärtig
currently [ˈkʌrəntli]	zurzeit
custom [ˈkʌstəm]	Einkauf
CV [,siː ˈviː]	Lebenslauf

D

to **damage** [ˈdæmɪdʒ]	schaden, beschädigen
dash [dæʃ]	Binde-, Gedankenstrich
deadline [ˈdedlaɪn]	Frist
to **deal in** [ˈdiːl ɪn]	handeln mit
decision [dɪˈsɪʒn]	Entscheidung
definite [ˈdefɪnət]	bestimmt, fest
delay [dɪˈleɪ]	Verspätung
to **delete** [dɪˈliːt]	löschen
deleted items [dɪˈliːtɪd aɪtəmz]	gelöschte Objekte
delivery [dɪˈlɪvəri]	Lieferung
dentist [ˈdentɪst]	Zahnarzt, Zahnärztin
to **depend on** [dɪˈpend ɒn]	abhängen von, sich verlassen auf
depending [dɪˈpendɪŋ]	abhängig
design [dɪˈzaɪn]	Entwurf, Konstruktion
despite this [dɪˈspaɪt ðɪs]	trotzdem
detail, in ~ [ɪn ˈdiːteɪl]	im Detail
to **dictate** [dɪkˈteɪt]	diktieren, bestimmen
diplomatic [,dɪpləˈmætɪk]	diplomatisch
direct [dəˈrekt]	direkt, gerade
distributor [dɪˈstrɪbjətə]	Lieferant
to **diversify** [daɪˈvɜːsɪfaɪ]	diversifizieren
division [dɪˈvɪʒn]	Abteilung
draft [draːft]	Entwurf
due: amount ~ [əˈmaʊnt ˈdjuː]	ausstehender Betrag
due to [ˈdjuː tə]	aufgrund

E

Easter [ˈiːstə]	Ostern
effective [ɪˈfektɪv]	wirkungsvoll
electronically [,ɪlekˈtrɒnɪkli]	elektronisch
engineering [,endʒɪˈnɪərɪŋ]	Technik, Maschinenbau
employee [ɪmˈplɔɪiː]	Mitarbeiter/in
to **encourage** [ɪnˈkʌrɪdʒ]	ermutigen, auffordern
to **enforce** [ɪnˈfɔːs]	durchsetzen
to **enquire** [ɪnˈkwaɪə]	erfragen
enquiry [ɪnˈkwaɪəri]	Anfrage, Frage
equivalent [ɪˈkwɪvələnt]	Entsprechung; entsprechend
etiquette [ˈetɪket]	Etikette
event [ɪˈvent]	Ereignis, Veranstaltung
examination [ɪg,zæmɪˈneɪʃn]	Prüfung, Examen
exciting [ɪkˈsaɪtɪŋ]	aufregend, spannend
exclamation mark [ekskləˈmeɪʃn maːk]	Ausrufezeichen

to **expect** [ɪk'spekt]		erwarten
extension [ɪk'stenʃn]		Verlängerung
extension number [ɪk'stenʃn nʌmbə]		Durchwahl(nummer)

F

familiar [fə'mɪlɪə]	vertraut
feature ['fi:tʃə]	Merkmal, Kennzeichen
feedback ['fi:dbæk]	Rückmeldung
figure ['fɪgə]	Zahl, Ziffer
filing cabinet ['faɪlɪŋ kæbɪnət]	Aktenschrank
to **finalize** ['faɪnəlaɪz]	endgültig festlegen
firm [fɜ:m]	Firma
first thing ['fɜ:st θɪŋ]	früh am Morgen
flyer ['flaɪə]	Flugblatt
to **follow up** ['fɒləʊ ˌʌp]	etw weiterverfolgen
formal ['fɔ:ml]	formell, förmlich
forward ['fɔ:wəd]	vorwärts
to **forward** ['fɔ:wəd]	(nach)senden
forwarder ['fɔ:wədə]	Spediteur
freephone ['fri:fəʊn]	gebührenfreies Telefon
full [fʊl]	voll
function ['fʌŋkʃn]	Funktion
furniture ['fɜ:nɪtʃə]	Möbel(stücke)
future ['fju:tʃə]	Zukunft; (zu)künftig

G

gently ['dʒentli]	sanft, leicht
golfer ['gɒlfə]	Golfer/in
goods [gʊdz]	Ware(n), Güter
government ['gʌvənmənt]	Regierung
granted, to be ~ [bi 'grɑ:ntɪd]	gestattet/erlaubt werden
grateful ['greɪtfl]	dankbar
greeting card ['gri:tɪŋ kɑ:d]	Glückwunschkarte
guest [gest]	Gast
guideline ['gaɪdlaɪn]	Richtlinie

H

handbook ['hændbʊk]	Bedienungsanleitung, Handbuch
hard copy [ˌhɑ:d 'kɒpi]	Ausdruck
headquarters [hed'kwɔ:təz]	Zentrale
heated ['hi:tɪd]	emotional
heavy ['hevi]	schwer, hoch, stark
hectic ['hektɪk]	hektisch
highly-qualified [ˌhaɪli 'kwɒlɪfaɪd]	hoch qualifiziert
hoax [həʊks]	Schwindel, Streich
however [haʊ'evə]	jedoch, aber
human resources [ˌhju:mən rɪ'sɔ:sɪz]	Personalabteilung
Hungarian [hʌŋ'geərɪən]	Ungar/in, ungarisch
hyphen ['haɪfn]	Bindestrich

I

immediate [ɪ'mi:dɪət]	sofortig, unmittelbar
imperative [ɪm'perətɪv]	Befehlsform
impersonal [ɪm'pɜ:sənl]	unpersönlich
inappropriate [ˌɪnə'prəʊprɪət]	unpassend, unangemessen
inbox ['ɪnbɒks]	Posteingang
to **include** [ɪn'klu:d]	einbeziehen, umfassen
including [ɪn'klu:dɪŋ]	einschließlich, inbegriffen
increase ['ɪŋkri:s]	Zunahme, Steigerung
to **infect** [ɪn'fekt]	infizieren, anstecken
to **inform** [ɪn'fɔ:m]	informieren, benachrichtigen,
initials [ɪ'nɪʃlz]	Initialen, Anfangsbuchstaben
input ['ɪnpʊt]	Eingabe
to **install** [ɪn'stɔ:l]	installieren, anschließen
internal [ɪn'tɜ:nl]	intern
Internet access [ˌɪntənet 'ækses]	Internet-Zugang
to **introduce** [ˌɪntrə'dju:s]	(sich) vorstellen, einführen
invitation [ˌɪnvɪ'teɪʃn]	Einladung
invoice ['ɪnvɔɪs]	Rechnung
involved [ɪn'vɒlvd]	beteiligt
issue ['ɪʃu:]	Frage, Thema

J

job application [dʒɒb ˌæplɪ'keɪʃn]	Stellenbewerbung

joke [dʒəʊk]	Witz, Scherz
junk mail ['dʒʌŋk meɪl]	Postwurfsendung(en)

K

to **keep an eye on** [ki:p ən 'aɪ ɒn]	ein (wachsames) Auge haben auf
knowledge ['nɒlɪdʒ]	Wissen, Kenntnis(se)

L

law [lɔ:]	Recht, Gesetz
leaflet ['li:flət]	Broschüre, Prospekt
limited ['lɪmɪtɪd]	beschränkt, begrenzt
location [ləʊ'keɪʃn]	Lage
to **log on** [ˌlɒg 'ɒn]	einloggen, anmelden
logical ['lɒdʒɪkl]	logisch
loop, to leave sb out of the ~ [ˌli:v aʊt əv ðə 'lu:p]	jdn ausschließen
lost [lɒst]	verloren
lounge [laʊndʒ]	Salon, Warteraum
low-down, the ~ ['ləʊdaʊn]	ausführliche Information
luggage ['lʌgɪdʒ]	Gepäck

M

mail box ['meɪl bɒks]	Mailbox, Briefkasten
mail shots ['meɪl ʃɒts]	(Post-)Wurfsendungen
majority [mə'dʒɒrəti]	Mehrheit
to **make (an appointment)** [ˌmeɪk ən ə'pɔɪntmənt]	(einen Termin) vereinbaren; einhalten
manual ['mænjʊəl]	Handbuch
market research [ˌmɑ:kɪt rɪ'sɜ:tʃ]	Marktforschung
medium-sized [ˌmi:dɪəm saɪzd]	mittelgroß
memo ['meməʊ]	Notiz, Kurzmitteilung
merger ['mɜ:dʒə]	Fusion, Zusammenschluss
minor ['maɪnə]	klein, geringfügig
minutes, the ~ ['mɪnɪts]	Protokoll
mistake [mɪ'steɪk]	Fehler, Irrtum
monitoring ['mɒnɪtərɪŋ]	Überwachung, Kontrolle
to **monitor** ['mɒnɪtə]	überwachen, kontrollieren
mother-in-law ['mʌðər ɪn lɔ:]	Schwiegermutter
mouse mat ['maʊs mæt]	Mousepad

N

native speaker [ˌneɪtɪv 'spi:kə]	Muttersprachler/in
necessary ['nesəsəri]	notwendig, erforderlich
negotiation [nɪˌgəʊʃi'eɪʃn]	Verhandlung
non-profit [ˌnɒn'prɒfɪt]	gemeinnützig
nowadays ['naʊədeɪz]	heutzutage

O

to **offend** [ə'fend]	beleidigen
offer ['ɒfə]	Angebot
official [ə'fɪʃl]	offiziell, amtlich
opinion [ə'pɪnɪən]	Meinung
order ['ɔ:də]	Bestellung
outbox ['aʊtbɒks]	Postausgang
outstanding [aʊt'stændɪŋ]	rückständig
overhead ['əʊvəhed]	Folie
to **overreact** [ˌəʊvərɪ'ækt]	überreagieren
overseas [ˌəʊvə'si:z]	ausländisch

P

packaging ['pækɪdʒɪŋ]	Verpackung
paperclip ['peɪpəklɪp]	Büroklammer
parking permit ['pɑ:kɪŋ pɜ:mɪt]	Parkgenehmigung
participant [pɑ:'tɪsɪpənt]	Teilnehmer/in
particular [pə'tɪkjələ]	bestimmt, speziell
to **pass on** [ˌpɑ:s 'ɒn]	weiterleiten
pay rise ['peɪ raɪz]	Gehaltserhöhung
percentage [pə'sentɪdʒ]	Prozentsatz
personal ['pɜ:sənl]	persönlich
pet hate ['pet heɪt]	Gräuel
petty cash [ˌpeti 'kæʃ]	Portokasse
phenomena [fə'nɒmɪnə]	Phänomene
to **pick sb up** [ˌpɪk 'ʌp]	jdn abholen
policy ['pɒləsi]	Politik, Police
polite [pə'laɪt]	höflich
popular ['pɒpjələ]	beliebt, populär
population [ˌpɒpju'leɪʃn]	Bevölkerung, Einwohner
positively ['pɒzətɪvli]	positiv
to **postpone** [pə'spəʊn]	verschieben

potential [pə'tenʃl]	möglich, potenziell
powerful ['pauəfl]	mächtig, stark
precaution [prɪ'kɔːʃn]	Vorsichtsmaßnahme
to **predict** [prɪ'dɪkt]	vorhersagen
presentation [ˌprezn'teɪʃn]	Vorführung, Vorstellung
to **prevent** [prɪ'vent]	(ver)hindern, verhüten
previously ['priːviəsli]	vorher
price increase ['praɪs ɪnkriːs]	Preiserhöhung
priority [praɪ'ɒrəti]	Vorrang, Priorität
privacy ['prɪvəsi]	Privatsphäre
probably ['prɒbəbli]	wahrscheinlich
to **process** ['prəʊses]	ver-, bearbeiten
product ['prɒdʌkt]	Produkt, Erzeugnis
product range ['prɒdʌkt reɪndʒ]	Produktpalette
production [prə'dʌkʃn]	Produktion, Herstellung
productivity [ˌprɒdʌk'tɪvəti]	Produktivität
promotion [prə'məʊʃn]	Werbung, Marketing
prompt [prɒmpt]	sofort, umgehend
to **propose** [prə'pəʊz]	vorschlagen
to **protect** [prə'tekt]	(be)schützen
punctuation [ˌpʌŋktʃu'eɪʃn]	Zeichensetzung
to **purchase** ['pɜːtʃəs]	einkaufen
purpose ['pɜːpəs]	Zweck, Ziel, Absicht
to **put off** [ˌpʊt 'ɒf]	verschieben

Q

quarter ['kwɔːtə]	Quartal, Viertel(jahr)
quarterly ['kwɔːtəli]	vierteljährlich
to **quote** [kwəʊt]	Kostenvoranschlag machen

R

radiator ['reɪdieɪtə]	Heizkörper, Kühler
range [reɪndʒ]	Sortiment
rather ['rɑːðə]	ziemlich, lieber
reason ['riːzn]	Grund
to **receive** [rɪ'siːv]	erhalten, bekommen
recently ['riːsntli]	vor kurzem
reception [rɪ'sepʃn]	Empfang, Rezeption
receptionist [rɪ'sepʃənɪst]	Empfangsmitarbeiter/in
recipient [rɪ'sɪpiənt]	Empfänger/in
to **reduce** [rɪ'djuːs]	reduzieren, senken
regards [rɪ'gɑːdz]	Grüße
to **regret** [rɪ'gret]	bedauern, bereuen
regulation [ˌregju'leɪʃn]	Bestimmung, Vorschrift
related [rɪ'leɪtɪd]	verwandt
remark [rɪ'mɑːk]	Bemerkung
to **remind** [rɪ'maɪnd]	(jdn an etw) erinnern
report [ˌrɪ'pɔːt]	Bericht
rep(resentative)	Vertreter/in
[ˌreprɪ'zentətɪv]	
to **represent** [ˌreprɪ'zent]	vertreten
reprinted, to be ~ [bi ˌriː'prɪntɪd]	nachgedruckt werden
request [rɪ'kwest]	Bitte, Anfrage, An-, Aufforderung
to **reschedule** [ˌriː'ʃedjuːl]	neu planen
research [rɪ'sɜːtʃ]	Forschung
to **reserve** [rɪ'zɜːv]	reservieren
resident ['rezɪdənt]	Ein-, Bewohner/in
response [rɪ'spɒns]	Antwort, Rückmeldung
retirement [rɪ'taɪəmənt]	(Eintritt in den) Ruhestand, Pensionierung
to **reveal** [rɪ'viːl]	enthüllen
to **rise** [raɪz]	(an)steigen, klettern
rustic ['rʌstɪk]	rustikal

S

safe [seɪf]	sicher
salutation [ˌsælju'teɪʃn]	Anrede
sample ['sɑːmpl]	Muster, Probe
sarcastic [sɑː'kæstɪk]	sarkastisch, ironisch
saw [sɔː]	Säge
scenario [sə'nɑːriəʊ]	Szenario
schedule ['ʃedjuːl]	Zeitplan
to **scrap** [skræp]	aufgeben
to **screen** [skriːn]	untersuchen, überprüfen
security [sɪ'kjʊərəti]	Sicherheit
sender name ['sendə neɪm]	Absender

seriously ['sɪəriəsli]	ernsthaft
service ['sɜːvɪs]	Kundendienst, Wartung
to **set up** [ˌset 'ʌp]	aufbauen, einrichten
sexual harassment [ˌsekʃuəl 'hærəsmənt]	sexuelle Belästigung
shocked [ʃɒkt]	schockiert
shouting ['ʃaʊtɪŋ]	Geschrei, Schreien
shower cabinet [ˌʃaʊə 'kæbɪnət]	Duschkabine
sick leave ['sɪk liːv]	Genesungsurlaub
to **sign up** [ˌsaɪn 'ʌp]	(sich) einschreiben
similarly ['sɪmələli]	ähnlich
slash [slæʃ]	Schrägstrich
slight [slaɪt]	gering, leicht
sloppy ['slɒpi]	nachlässig, salopp
snail-mail ['sneɪl meɪl]	Schneckenpost
sophisticated [sə'fɪstɪkeɪtɪd]	differenziert, kompliziert
to **sort out** [ˌsɔːt 'aʊt]	klären, lösen
spam [spæm]	unangeforderte Werbe-Email
specific [spə'sɪfɪk]	speziell, spezifisch
spelling ['spelɪŋ]	Rechtschreibung
standstill ['stændstɪl]	Stillstand
stationery ['steɪʃənri]	Briefpapier, Büromaterial
stats (statistics) [stæts, stə'tɪstɪks]	Statistiken
stock, in ~ [ɪn 'stɒk]	vorrätig
to **store** [stɔː]	speichern, aufbewahren
straight away [streɪt ə'weɪ]	sofort, auf der Stelle, umgehend
strict [strɪkt]	streng
strike [straɪk]	Streik
structure ['strʌktʃə]	Struktur, Aufbau
subject line ['sʌbdʒɪkt laɪn]	Bezugs-, Betreffzeile
successful [sək'sesfl]	erfolgreich
survey ['sɜːveɪ]	Umfrage, Übersicht
suspicious [sə'spɪʃəs]	verdächtig, misstrauisch

T

task [tɑːsk]	Aufgabe
tap [tæp]	(Wasser-)Hahn
terms and conditions [ˌtɜːmz ənd kən'dɪʃnz]	allgemeine Geschäftsbedingungen
tool [tuːl]	Werkzeug
totally ['təʊtəli]	völlig, total, komplett
to **touch base** [tʌtʃ 'beɪs]	in Kontakt treten
touch, to get in ~ [get ɪn 'tʌtʃ]	in Kontakt treten
towel rail ['taʊəl reɪl]	Handtuchhalter
trade fair ['treɪd feə]	Handelsmesse
transferred, to be ~ [bi træns'fɜːd]	versetzt werden
travel expenses ['trævl ɪkspensɪz]	Reisekosten
typical ['tɪpɪkl]	typisch

U

underscore [ˌʌndə'skɔː]	Unterstreichung
unfortunately [ʌn'fɔːtʃənətli]	leider
unknown [ˌʌn'nəʊn]	unbekannt
unusual [ʌn'juːʒʊəl]	ungewöhnlich
unwanted [ˌʌn'wɒntɪd]	unerwünscht
upcoming ['ʌpkʌmɪŋ]	kommend, bevorstehend
to **update sb** [ˌʌp'deɪt]	jdm erzählen, was neu ist
urgent ['ɜːdʒənt]	dringend

V

to **vary** ['veəri]	sich unterscheiden, variieren
venue ['venjuː]	(Veranstaltungs-)Ort
vicinity, in the ~ [ɪn ðə və'sɪnəti]	in der Nähe
virus detection software [ˌvaɪrəs dɪ'tekʃn sɒftweə]	Virenschutzprogramme
voicemail ['vɔɪsmeɪl]	Mailbox

W

warehouse ['weəhaʊs]	Lager(halle)
warning ['wɔːnɪŋ]	Warnung
to **wonder** ['wʌndə(r)]	sich fragen
worried ['wʌrid]	besorgt, beunruhigt

Useful phrases and vocabulary

The phrases on pages 62–63 are colour-coded according to how formal they are:

blue = more formal   **black = standard**   **green = (very) informal**

Please note that this is only an approximate guide. Whether a phrase is too formal or too informal often depends on the context of the email and your personal writing style.

Salutations

When you don't know the name:
Dear Sir or Madam
To whom it may concern
Hello
[no salutation]

When you know the name:
Dear Mr, Mrs, Ms ...
Dear John
Hello Pat
Hi Mary
Hey John
Mira
[no salutation]

When writing to a group:
Dear all
Hi everyone

Opening sentence

Replying to an email:
Thanks (very much) for your email.
This is to say thanks for your email.

Giving a reason:

I'm (just) writing to ...	clarify ...
Just a (quick) note to ...	confirm ...
Just a short email to ...	inform you...
	follow up on ...
	let you know ...
	reply to ...
	request ...
	tell you ...
	thank you ...
	update you ...

Attaching files

I'm sending you/attaching ...
I've attached ...
Please find attached ...
I'm sending you the price list/document as an attachment.

When things go wrong:
I'm afraid you forgot to attach the file/...
I'm afraid I can't open the file/document. Can/Could you send it again in ... format, please?

Making enquiries

I am interested in receiving/finding out ...
I would like to receive ...
We would be grateful if ...
Could/Can you please send me ... ?
Please send me ...
Would you be able to (help) ... ?
Can you help?
I'd appreciate a reply asap.
Please answer asap.

Replying to an enquiry

Thank you for your interest.
I'm pleased to send you ...
I'm sending you ... (in an attachment)
Please find the requested information attached.
We hope you find this satisfactory.
We hope you are happy/satisfied with this.
Thanks for choosing ...

When there will be a delay:
Your request is being processed.
We are working on your request.

Informing

I'd like to inform you of ...
Just a few comments about your last mail:
I'm writing to tell you about/let you know ...
Just a note to say ...
Here's the low-down on ...
Just to update you on ...
FYI: This is to let you know ...
Hope this helps.
Let me/us know if you need anything else.

Requesting action

Have you ... yet?
Can you send ... to me by Friday, please?
I need ... by Thursday.
Please get/keep in touch.
Keep me posted.

Replying

Thanks for your email …
In reply to your email, here are …
Re your email, I …
You'll find the info(rmation) attached.
I'll get back to you asap …
I'll follow up the points mentioned in your email …

Making arrangements

Just a quick note to arrange a time to meet.
I'm writing to set up/arrange …
How/What about Tuesday?
Is … OK?
Where should we meet?
Should I pick you up at/from … ?
Could you collect me at … ?

Confirming arrangements

I'd like to confirm …
Just writing to confirm …
Tuesday is good for me.
Please send me an email by 5 pm today to confirm this.
Looking forward to seeing/meeting …

Changing arrangements

I'm sorry but I can't do/make Thursday.
This is to let you now that I've had to put off/postpone …
I'm writing to call off/cancel …
I'm afraid I can't make/manage Friday. How about … instead?

Giving good news

I am/We are pleased to inform you …
I'm happy to tell you …
You'll be happy/delighted to hear that …

Giving bad news

We regret to tell/inform you …
I'm sorry, but …
I am afraid that …
Unfortunately, …

Complaining

I'm writing to complain (about …).
We're not happy with …
I was disappointed to find/hear …
I'm afraid that …
Unfortunately, …

Apologizing

For a delay in answering:
I do apologize for the delay in replying.
Sorry for the delay in getting back to you.
Sorry this is so late.

For not being able to help:
Sorry, I don't know.
I'm afraid I can't help you.

For something more serious:
We must apologize for …
We deeply regret …
My sincere apologies (*close*)
We apologize for any inconvenience caused.
Please accept our apologies.
I'm so sorry …

Friendly ending

When you want a reply:
I look forward/Looking forward to hearing from you/to your reply.
Hope to hear from you soon.
I'd appreciate a reply asap.

Offering more help:
Do not hesitate to contact us if you need any assistance.
Feel free to get in touch …
    if you have any other questions
    if you need more help.
    with any questions.
Let me know if you need anything else/if I can help you further.

General:
Thanks for your help/cooperation.
Hope all is well with you.
Have a nice day/weekend! :-)

Close

Yours sincerely
Kind/Best regards
Regards
Best wishes
All the best
Best
See you (soon)
Take care
Bye (for now)
[just the name or initials]
[no close]

Useful verbs (in context)

to apologize	I'd like to apologize for any inconvenience caused.	entschuldigen
to appreciate	We'd appreciate a reply … /I'd appreciate it if you could send me …	dankbar sein für
to arrange	I'm writing to arrange a meeting … /Can you arrange for somebody to collect me …?	arrangieren
to ask (if)	Could I ask you to send me … ?/This is to ask if you could …	fragen
to assist	Please let us know if we can assist you in any way.	helfen
to clarify	I am writing to clarify the terms of the agreement.	klarstellen
to complain	I'm writing to complain about …/I'm afraid I must complain about …	sich beschweren
to confirm	I'd like to confirm my booking/the date of our next meeting.	bestätigen
to contact	Please contact Mr … at our London office.	Kontakt aufnehmen
to enquire	I'd like to enquire about …	erfragen
to follow up	Just wanted to follow up on that unpaid invoice.	etw weiterfolgen
to get in touch	Please get in touch (with me) asap.	in Kontakt treten
to inform	FYI: This is to inform you that …/inform you of a problem …	informieren
to let sb know	Can you let me know the price of … ?/This is to let you know that we …	jdm Bescheid sagen
to need	I need those figures on my desk before tomorrow's meeting.	brauchen
to postpone	I'm afraid we've had to postpone the conference.	verschieben
to put off	Sorry, but we're going to have to put off the meeting till next week.	verscheiben
to receive	We've just received the invoice …	erhalten
to regret	We regret to inform you that …	bedauern
to reply	I am writing to reply to your enquiry about …	antworten
to send	We are sending you the handbook as an attachment.	schicken
to sort out	Please can you sort out the mess with the accounts!	klären, lösen
to touch base	Just wanted to touch base with you before the meeting.	in Kontakt treten
to update	This is to update you on the Johnson account.	erzählen, was neu ist
to write	I'm writing to let you know …	schreiben

Abbreviations and acronyms

Common abbreviations:

& (ampersand)	and
+	and/plus
ad(vert)	advertisement
am	in the morning
appt	appointment
asap	as soon as possible
at the mo	at the moment
eg	for example
etc	etcetera/and so on
ie	in other words
info	information
pls	please
pm	in the afternoon
re	regarding/about
rep	representative
rgds	regards
w/e	weekend
wk	week
yr	year/your

Mon	Monday
Tues	Tuesday
Wed	Wednesday
Thurs	Thursday
Fri	Friday
Sat	Saturday
Sun	Sunday

Jan	January
Feb	February
Mar	March
Apr	April
May	May
Jun	June
Jul	July
Aug	August
Sept	September
Oct	October
Nov	November
Dec	December

Email, chatroom and text-messaging:

FAQ	Frequently asked questions
Thx	thanks
TIA	thanks in advance
IMO	in my opinion
CU	see you
FYI	for your information
BTW	by the way
Fwd	forward
LOL	laughing out loud
2	to
U	you
RU	are you